Foul Deeds and Suspicious De

DURHAM

MAUREEN ANDERSON

Series Editor
Brian Elliott

Wharncliffe Books

First Published in 2003 and reprinted in 2012 by
Wharncliffe Books
an imprint of
Pen and Sword Books Limited,
47 Church Street, Barnsley,
South Yorkshire. S70 2AS

*For up-to-date information on other titles produced under the
Wharncliffe imprint, please telephone or write to:*

Wharncliffe Books
FREEPOST
47 Church Street
Barnsley
South Yorkshire S70 2BR
Telephone (24 hours): 01226 734555

ISBN: 1-903425-46-8

A CIP catalogue record of this book is available from the
British Library

Cover illustration:
Front – *'La Meurte' (The Murder) by Paul Cezanne, 1868. Liverpool Walker Art Gallery*
Rear – *The altar tomb of the Brass children, Kirk Merrington. The author*

Printed in the United Kingdom by
CPI Group (UK) Ltd, Croydon, CR0 4YY

Contents

Introduction

Durham – Land of the Prince Bishops – holds a unique place in the annals of history relating to counties within England. From the middle ages the county was in the hands of the Bishops of Durham. They ruled over both the religious and state affairs within their borders. The diocese was very wealthy, owning valuable land and mineral rights. The mid-nineteenth century saw the dismantling of the Palatinate and many of the county's assets were distributed throughout the Church of England and the diocese split.

In 1974 drastic boundary changes were implemented on County Durham. Sunderland, Gateshead and towns on the south bank of the Tyne became part of the new county of Tyne and Wear and the county of Cleveland was formed. The events in this book took place in some of the towns and villages that were part of Durham before the boundary changes.

It is probable that the Romans excavated for coal in Durham. The earliest record of coal mining here was recorded in the eleventh century in the Boldon Book when a miner supplied coal from Escomb to Coundon. By the early nineteenth century coal mines had sprung up all over Durham and families from the southern parts of England and from Ireland had arrived in their thousands seeking work. Records show there were 154,000 employed in the collieries within the area. Small existing villages and towns expanded to become host to the mineworkers and their families and new villages and towns were born. Many of these families had lived in abject poverty prior to the coal-mining boom. Now they found themselves with a little money, but sadly, instead of providing a better way of life for themselves, some of them spent their wages on alcohol. Along with the drink came domestic violence, cruelty and drunken brawls, often resulting in death. Women and children were not held in high esteem. Often the partner or spouse, sometimes because of suspected infidelity, whether real or imagined, became the victim of drunken rage. Throughout the nineteenth and twentieth centuries there were ninety-three recorded hangings in Durham. A large proportion of these were for the murder of a partner. Many of the murders related in these chapters resulted in the ultimate penalty of hanging.

Prior to the mid-nineteenth century, executions were carried out for almost any offence, including rape, the stealing of livestock or robbery. As a warning to others the body of a murderer would sometimes be hung in chains and left on display at or near to where the crime took place. Some of the executions were carried out with almost as much cruelty as the criminal had inflicted on the victim.

Although still far from perfect, the justice system has changed radically over the centuries. Once controlled largely by ignorance and superstition, the execution of a 'witch' could be carried out with the finger of guilt pointed at someone because of the failure of crops, livestock becoming ill or even hens not laying. Conviction for a crime often relied on the statements of witnesses as to the suspect's movements prior to and after the deed was committed. Gradually, forensic evidence has become more of an exact science helping to protect the innocent and convict the guilty.

Readers are left to make up their own minds as to whether justice was properly served in the sentences passed down in these events. Or, indeed, whether the person charged was really the guilty party.

Finding out how our ancestors lived and the genealogy of our families has become increasingly popular in recent years. Perhaps you have traced your family line to a certain point and been able to go no further? Well, it could be possible that the trail may have ended because your ancestor was a victim, or even perhaps the perpetrator of a crime who was hanged, imprisoned or transported by way of punishment.

Foul Deeds and Suspicious Deaths In & Around Durham, published by Wharncliffe Books, is part of an ever-growing series relating to different towns and areas of England. The series looks into the darker side of our history and heritage.

These are some of the lesser-known events that have been all but forgotten through time and now unearthed through research of historical manuscripts, and newspapers. They have come together to show not only 'the evil that men do' but also the seedier side of life in the small cramped houses, public bars and streets in the towns and villages of County Durham.

My sincere gratitude to Wharncliffe Books for giving me the opportunity to write a second book for the *Foul Deeds and Suspicious Deaths* series and to the Series Editor, Brian Elliott, for his invaluable suggestions and assistance. Also my thanks to all the staff of the Hartlepool Reference Library and to my partner, Jim, who has always, in every project I have undertaken, encouraged me from beginning to end.

I would also like to acknowledge the following for their assistance with illustrations: The Arts and History Picture Library, Bowes Museum, Durham Mining Museum, Durham Federation of Women's Institutes, Countryside Books, Brian Elliott, Howard Clough and John 'Harry' Harrison.

Chapter 1

Before 1800

Blackwell, 1624

Christopher Simpson was an elderly labourer from Thornaby. On Thursday, 3 June 1624, he travelled to Aldborough in Richmondshire to the house of a weaver, Ralph Simpson, who was a kinsman (probably a nephew) and friend. After the two men had exchanged pleasantries for a while, they agreed to go to Gunnersfield on the following day to visit another friend, John Metcalfe. Christopher was riding a bay mare so it seems that Ralph would also have been on horseback. On arriving at Gunnersfield, Ralph conducted some business with John. When the two men left to return home on the Saturday, Ralph had a little black mare and ten shillings (50p) from John. Presumably, he had traded the mare and the money for the horse he had been riding. On arriving at Richmond, before going home,

Blackwell Gate, Darlington in the late nineteenth century. Author's collection

Darlington from the east in the eighteenth century. Author's collection

Ralph bought a pair of boots.

Late that Saturday night Christopher's body was found on the side of the road at Baydale Bank, within the territory of Blackwell in the parish of Darlington. His neck showed signs of him having been strangled with a thin cord. The people of Blackwell who found the body sent immediately for the deputy coroner and a rider was sent to Aldborough to bring Ralph Simpson to the scene. Fourteen jurors were sworn and the funeral and the inquest were held on the Sunday at the place where the murder was committed.

Ralph's story was, that after calling at Richmond, Christopher had left his bay mare with him saying that the horse was tired. Christopher had then left and Ralph said he had not seen his kinsman again. Witnesses came forward to say they had seen the two men riding together on Saturday night after the time Ralph had said that they parted company. Bartholomew Harrison of

Countscliffe stated that he had seen Ralph before sunrise on that morning (Sunday) near to where the body was found. Ralph denied this, saying that at the time he had being going to Darlington to buy boots. The deputy coroner and a constable, Thomas Emmerson, searched Ralph's pockets and found a cord (the ends of a weaver's web). The cord was covered in fresh, undried blood. Ralph was asked why he had the cord and he replied that he used it to tie his wallet. As to where the blood had come from, Ralph had no answer. The cord was placed in the groove on Christopher's neck and was found to fit perfectly. The men of the jury then questioned why Ralph would be going to Darlington to buy boots when he had just purchased a pair in Richmond. The final proof came to the jurors when Ralph was ordered to handle the body:

> *And wee caused the said Raph to handle the bodye; and upon his handlings and movings, the bodye did bleed both at mouth, nose and eares.*
>
> *Wee the jurye do find and think that Raph Simpson, weaver, haith by the instigation of the Devell or of some secret malice, murdered and strangled Christopher Simpson at and in the place of ground commonly known as Baydayle Banckes Head, it being the fift day of June at night, this present year 1624.*

Richmond in the early twentieth century. Elijah Yeoman, Bowes Museum

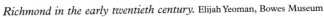

The Unicorn, *Richmond, an old coaching inn, parts of which date from the sixteenth century.* Howard Clough

The records then relate that Ralph was escorted to Durham gaol. His fate was not recorded but he would certainly have been hanged.

At the time, the Baydayle Banckes Tragedy became the subject of many a ballad:

> *Oh Blackwell is a lovesome vill! And Baydayle Banckes are bright!*
> *The Sabbath breeze the crystal Tees with wavelets has bedight;*
> *Come tell me child, my Averil mild, why harried thus you be?*
> *Father, there is a murdered man beneath yon greenwood tree.*
> *Ho! neighbours mine, here Cornforth bold, and Middleton of might,*
> *For there hath been a slaughter foul, at Baydayle Head last night.*

Highway robbery was a common crime on the lonely cart tracks and footpaths so Christopher could have been attacked with robbery as a motive. There was no way of proving that whatever was on the cord Ralph was carrying was indeed blood. Witnesses were not always reliable as to times, as time was told by the setting and rising of the sun. No motive for Ralph committing the murder was recorded but whether he was guilty or not he was convicted on hearsay and superstition.

Lumley, 1631:

Whether or not one believes in ghosts and the supernatural, this strange event was recorded by the eminent historian, Robert Surtees, so must have been thought worthy of belief.

John Walker was a wealthy yeoman living at Lumley, near Chester-le-Street. Being a widower, he employed Anne Walker, a young kinswoman of his, to keep house for him. Anne became pregnant but although she did not disclose who had fathered the baby, the events that followed pointed to John Walker. As her condition became more obvious, she was sent to live with an aunt, Dame Caire, in the same town.

After Anne had been staying with Dame Caire for some time a man visited her one night. He was Mark Sharp, a collier from Lancashire and a 'sworn brother' to Walker. Sharp took Anne from the house and she never returned.

Two miles from Lumley, James Graham (or Grime) worked as a miller. About fourteen days after Anne's disappearance, Graham began to be plagued by visions. He was working alone late one night grinding corn. After having put the corn in the hopper, Graham came downstairs. The mill doors were shut but in the middle of the floor there was a woman standing. Her hair was hanging down and covered with blood. The apparition had five wounds to her head and when asked what she wanted, she declared that she was the spirit of Anne Walker. The ghostly woman then told Graham that Anne had worked for a kinsman

Lumley Castle and the River Wear. Author's collection

called Walker and she had conceived by him. Walker had told Anne that he would take her to a private place where she would be well looked after. When her confinement was over and she was well again Anne could then return and keep house as before. The two men had then come for Anne in the night and taken her to a place that Graham knew. Sharp had then murdered her with a coal pick and put her body into a coal pit. The pick was then hidden under a bank along with his bloody shoes and stockings. Sharp had attempted to wash the blood from these but could not do so. The spirit then told Graham that if he did not reveal her story she would continue to haunt him. Graham, although sad and worried about what he had seen, kept quiet. Twice more the ghostly spectre visited Graham becoming more threatening each time. On the third visit Graham went to a justice of the peace and related his story. The justice ordered a search of the place that had been named. After a very short time Anne's body was found in a coal pit. There were five wounds to her head. Near to where her body was found were a pick and bloody shoes and stockings belonging to Sharp.

John Walker and Mark Sharp were apprehended and stood trial before Judge Davenport at the Durham Assizes. They were found guilty of murder and executed in August 1631.

Surtees wrote that in letters written by Mr Smart and Mr Lumley of Chester-le-Street there were some conflicting details relating to this story. In the main, however, the letters and records that were written at the time were in agreement, so he had no doubt that the events really took place.

Ferryhill, 1683:

John and Margaret Brass and their three children lived at Brass Farm near Ferryhill. They had a daughter, Jane, who was twenty and about to be married, a son, John who was seventeen and a younger daughter, Elizabeth, who was about eleven. John Brass employed Andrew Millns or Mills as a servant. Mills was a quiet inoffensive lad of eighteen or nineteen years of age with low intellect.

The Christmas celebrations for the family must have lasted well into January, because the master and mistress had gone away on a Christmas visit and had left Mills and the children at the

farm. On 25 January 1683, a bleak winter's day, Margaret and John Brass arrived back at the house, no doubt expecting a warm homecoming from their family. The horror of the sight that greeted them is unimaginable. Two bloodstained axes lay amongst the bloody and mutilated bodies of their three children.

Mills, by his own confession, had murdered them for no reason except that 'the enemy had suggested it'; the 'enemy' being the devil that had appeared to him in bodily form. His statement as to what had occurred was that he had been told to kill the family so he had entered the house brandishing an axe and had begun his attack. The records on which of the elder children was his first victim are conflicting. One record states that the slaughter began with John. There would have been little the youth could have done to protect himself against such a surprising and crazed onslaught. After Mills had felled John he then cut his throat. The elder girl, Jane, knowing that she and her sister were in mortal danger, went to the bedroom where Elizabeth was sleeping and placed her arm across the door to act as a bolt to keep Mills from entering the room. This was no deterrent to the crazed young man. Mills swung the axe at the door and broke Jane's arm. He then murdered her in the same way as he had her brother. Another record states that Jane was attacked first and John and Elizabeth were both in the bedroom. Jane ran to the bedroom door to protect both her younger brother and sister. Mills murdered Jane and then entered the bedroom and killed John. The records coincide as to what occurred next.

Mills had, reputably, been close to the youngest child, perhaps because of his own childish mentality. It may have been because of this friendship that, in his statement, Mills said he was then about to leave the house. Perhaps for a short while sanity and compassion took over, but whatever the reason, it was not to last. A voice or an impulse came into his head telling him to spare none and bidding him to 'Kill all, kill all'. Elizabeth, by this time, was awake and cowering under the bed in abject terror. Mills entered the room, dragged the screaming child from her hiding place and performed his bloody task for the third time. Mills then left the scene of carnage and ran through the village, his clothes covered in blood. He was soon arrested and sent to trial.

At his trial Mills stated that the acts had been committed because of voices and an apparition telling him to carry out the slaughter. Certainly there seemed, on the face of it, no cause for the servant to exact revenge. There can only be conjecture as to the motive. It was fairly common for menial servants to be treated with contempt by their employers. Perhaps because Mills was slow witted, his employers abused or took advantage of him. Perhaps he was enamoured with Jane and was jealous that she was marrying another young man. Nothing had been stolen so it was not for greed.

Mills was found guilty of murder because he had been in league with the devil. It was strongly believed by the self-righteous and the church that the devil could not enter a person's mind or body unless invited to do so. Therefore, Mills was considered insane but evil. If these events had taken place a century or so later his life would probably have been spared and he would have been committed to an asylum.

Mills was executed on 15 August 1683 on a common by the roadside, his body was then hung in chains and left to nature to dispose of. The place of his execution was about a half-mile north of Ferryhill in full view of the place where the murders were carried out. A portion of the gibbet, known as Andrew Mills' stob, remained for a few years after until the land was ploughed and enclosed. In commemoration of the tragic slaughter of the three children, an altar tomb was erected in Merrington churchyard. The tomb was restored by subscription in 1789.

Stories still live on in Ferryhill. It is said that the ghosts of the victims and the perpetrator haunt the area around the farm, especially near the old windmill. The windmill was not built until 1840 so did not exist at the time of the murders but perhaps it was at that spot in the field Mills had his first communication with the devil! Legend has it that Mills was tortured in an iron cage for several days and that he was already

The ruin of the windmill that is said to be haunted by the ghosts of the Brass children and Andrew Mills. The author

St John's Church, Kirk Merrington, where the Brass children and their parents are buried. The author

dead when he was hanged, but there is no real evidence of this. Someone, however, at some time scratched the word 'executed' from the children's tomb. Perhaps that person knew that Mills had not met his death by hanging. Over two hundred years after this terrible event the inscription on the murdered children's altar is almost indecipherable but it once read:

HERE LIE THE BODIES OF
JOHN, JANE AND ELIZABETH
CHILDREN OF
JOHN AND MARGARET BRASS
WHO WERE MURDERED THE 25TH OF JANUARY 1683
BY ANDREW MILLS, THEIR FATHER'S SERVANT
FOR WHICH HE WAS EXECUTED AND HUNG IN CHAINS
READER, REMEMBER, SLEEPING
WE WERE SLAIN,
AND HERE WE MUST SLEEP TIL
WE MUST RISE AGAIN.
WHOSO SHEDDETH MAN'S BLOOD BE SHED
THOU SHALT DO NO MURDER.
RESTORED BY SUBSCRIPTION IN 1789

The altar tomb of the three murdered Brass children in Kirk Merrington churchyard.
The author

Sunderland Docks painted in 1840 by Thomas Allom. Author's collection

Sunderland, 1745:

Mr Thomas Alder, a farmer at Hilton Park House, was walking in his fields when he was knocked down, his throat cut from ear to ear and his belly ripped open. Mr Alder's servant, as he was carrying milk to the farm, saw the murder. The perpetrator threatened to kill him also. The servant took to his heels and ran to Sunderland. When he returned with assistance the murderer was standing over the body and threatened anyone who came near him with death. The servant brought the murderer down with a stone and his helpers managed to secure him.

The murderer was Nicholas Haddock, a keelman from Sunderland. He stated that he had no malice against Alder and indeed, had never even seen or met him before that day. Haddock was found guilty and hanged on 26 August. Before he took his final breath he expressed his penitence and said he was distracted at the time of the fatal deed.

Whickham Common, 1750:

James MacFidum, alias MacFarlane, was executed at Durham on 27 August for robbing Robert Hopes, a boy of ten. He died penitent but expressing his innocence to being involved in the crime.

A sketch of Whickham Church in 1836. Author's collection

On 8 January 1750 young Robert was on his way to school and was crossing Whickham Common. He came upon a man with a woman sitting on his knee. The woman asked Robert where he was going. He replied that he was going to school. The man jumped up and grabbed Robert taking him into an adjoining hollow. The man then stripped the youngster of all his clothes except his breeches and shoes. While the man was doing this he was threatening Robert that he would cut his throat if he cried out. The boy managed to escape and ran to where his father was working not far away. Mr Hopes and some of the neighbours managed to pursue and capture MacFidum and take him to Reverend Mr Lamb who had him committed to Durham gaol. MacFidum maintained that he was dumb but Robert reminded him that he had a voice when he was using threats. MacFidum and the woman that was with him were thought to be part of a gang of Faws (rogues and robbers) that had, for many years, infested the neighbourhood.

Was this just a young boy's fanciful story or was MacFidum guilty?

Gateshead Fell, 1765:

William Middleton was a schoolmaster at the free school in Hartlepool and as such was well respected. His health, however, was poor and he was subject to fits. On 13 April, a cold and wet afternoon, Middleton was crossing Gateshead Fell on his way to Newcastle when he was attacked. Two men and a boy forced him into a quarry and threatened to kill him. Middleton, in his fear, lapsed into a fit, which made it very easy for the villains to carry out their evil designs. They stripped the helpless man of all his clothes, except for his stockings, leaving him exposed to the severity of the weather. The rain falling on his near naked body soon revived him but he was too cold and numb to move.

A cottager of the Fell was passing by when he saw a horse, saddled but with no rider, at the edge of the quarry. This aroused his suspicions as to all being not well. The cottager went into the quarry to investigate and finding Middleton unable to move or speak, the good neighbour carried the helpless man to a house nearby and put him to bed. People from the surrounding cottages went in search of the villains but they were never found. Eventually, Middleton recovered but remembered nothing of what had taken place after he was forced into the quarry. The victim complained of having a pain in his breast. One of the cottagers gave Middleton some clothes to wear and he went on his way.

Harraton, 1767:

On 13 February 1767 Ann Wilson took up an axe. Her husband was sitting in a chair by the fireside, sleeping. Ann crept up behind him and struck him on the side of the neck with all the force she could muster. Although his gullet was cut through and he was already dying, the wounded man jumped up in horror and pain. Ann then wielded the axe again caving in the poor man's head. He fell to the ground dying a few seconds later. Ann was confined in Durham gaol until the Autumn Assizes. In August of that year she was found guilty but insane.

Houghton le Spring, 1768:

Mr Easterby, a gentleman, and his servant were riding home to Farrington Hall from Sunderland on 17 June 1768. Four soldiers stopped them near the turnpike. One of the soldiers attacked Mr Easterby with a bayonet and robbed him of £1 5s (£1.25p). Luckily the gentleman was wearing a thick coat, so although stabbed in several places, was not mortally wounded. The servant, in defence of his master, struck and wounded the soldier in the face but as he did so was knocked from his horse. The servant managed to recover himself and went straight to Sunderland to tell one of the regiment's officers of the events that had taken place. An immediate search of the soldier's quarters was carried out to see who was absent. It was ascertained that the four involved were John Slaid, George Forster, John Adams and Thomas Croaker. The four returned to their quarters some short time later and were arrested. Slaid was bleeding profusely from a wound to his face. They were interrogated and eventually confessed to the crime. All four were severely flogged and then turned over to the civil power for

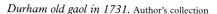

Durham old gaol in 1731. Author's collection

Sunderland Road, the main thoroughfare from Houghton le Spring to Sunderland in the early twentieth century. Author's collection

sentencing. Forster and Croaker were reprieved but Slaid and Adams received the sentence of death. Slaid confessed that it was he alone who had carried out the crime but he blamed his three companions for leading him astray. Adams was then also reprieved. Slaid was executed on 12 August 1768.

Gateshead Fell, 1770:
Miss Margaret Banson was sister to Mr Banson who was the writing master of the Newcastle Free Grammar School. Miss Banson had been to Durham on business and was returning in a post-chaise at about nine in the evening on 6 August. As they were travelling over Gateshead Fell a highwayman brandishing a pistol stopped the driver on pain of death. Upon the robber demanding money from Miss Banson, she, overcoming her fears, argued with the man. She told him that she only had half

a guinea (55p) and a halfpenny left. The man took the half guinea and then demanded her watch. With some difficulty Miss Banson convinced him that she did not have a watch and the man let the post-chaise go on its way. Miss Banson later stated that the robber had neither a greatcoat nor boots on; that he was badly mounted on his horse and had a great 'tremor' all the while. About a mile down the road they came upon the postman carrying the mail from Newcastle to Durham. Miss Banson told him of the highwayman and suggested that the postman either return to Newcastle or take a guard. The postman did not heed her advice but as he came to the turnpike gate he asked for a pistol. He did not manage to get one so went on his way unarmed.

A little further on from the gate the postman met a fellow

Grey Street, Newcastle in the nineteenth century. Author's collection

whom he assumed to be a countryman coming from the market. The two men rode on together for a while with the postman telling his companion about the robbery and that he did not manage to obtain a pistol to defend himself. In a soft voice the stranger told the postman that he must have his bags. The postman laughed, thinking it was a joke. His companion then pulled out a pistol and told the postman to alight from his horse and throw the mailbags onto the ground. The robber then told the postman to get back on his horse and ride away or he would blow his brains out.

The next day a man calling himself Robert Hazlitt, (otherwise William Hudson), who was in the company of a young woman, was arrested on suspicion of being the highwayman. Hazlitt said that he had been a clerk to Mr Samuel Bamford of Phillip Lane in London. He admitted to robbing Miss Banson but said it was an accomplice of his who had robbed the postman. Hazlitt said his accomplice, Hewitt, also from London, had brought the mailbags to a quarry. The two men had divided the spoils and Hazlitt had not seen Hewitt since.

Upon a search being carried out, many of the letters and bills were found in a chest. The young woman that was with Hazlitt said the chest belonged to her. On contacting Sir John Fielding in London, Hewitt was apprehended but it was found he had been in London at the time of the robberies. It was ascertained that Hazlitt had come from London by sea a day or two before the robberies. When he arrived he had hired a horse from Shields. It was thought this had been for the specific purpose of carrying out highway robberies.

Hazlitt was tried for the robbery of the post-chaise on 16 August and found guilty. He was then tried for robbing the mail and also found guilty. When the trials were over Hazlitt sent the judge some bills that he had secreted in his coat sleeve. He said that it was the money from the mailbags and the rest of the letters were in a cornfield. All the letters were found at the spot indicated.

Hazlitt's execution was carried out on 18 September near Durham. After hanging for two and a half hours, his body was cut down. He was then taken in a cart to a gibbet twenty-five feet high and hung in chains overlooking the place where the

Durham Banks in 1781. Author's collection

robberies were committed. There had been no order in Hazlitt's sentence that he should be hung in chains.

Soon after the body was hung in chains an elderly man was seen kneeling in front of the gibbet. This went on for several days, with the man kneeling there for some considerable time, even in wet weather. One day the man prostrated himself and became so enfeebled he could not rise. Upon some people assisting him from the ground, he drew a hatband out of his pocket, put it on, said he was now easy and then left the gruesome scene. It was believed that the old man was the dead man's father.

Chapter 2

False Evidence
1815

In the early hours of the morning of 28 August 1815, a fire was discovered raging through a house in Herrington. The house belonged to Miss Jane Smith. (Miss Smith later became Lady Peat when she married Reverend Sir Robert Peat, the chaplain and companion of George IV.) Miss Smith was away from home at the time but there was a servant girl, Isabella Young, staying in the house. The fire was brought under control before it reached Isabella, but she was already dead. Her body was found lying in the passage that led to the kitchen. She had two wounds to the back of her head and a large wound to the front. The body was nearly naked, so Isabella had probably been in bed and woken by some sound, had risen to investigate. It was obvious that the intruder or intruders, had been in the act of burglary when she had disturbed them. Isabella had been murdered and the fire had been lit to cover any trace of what had occurred.

When, after a period of time, no one was arrested, a reward was offered. A seaman of Sunderland, James Lincoln, came forward as a witness. On 13 August 1819, John Eden, James Wolfe and his son George, were put on trial for arson, burglary and murder. After a deliberation of nine hours by a jury, James Wolfe and John Eden were found guilty of the crimes. They were

Herrington Hall, now demolished. Author's collection

sentenced to be hanged on 16 August.

Some members of the Society of Friends (Quakers) who knew the men, took it upon themselves to conduct further investigations. Numerous affidavits were procured giving James Wolfe an alibi. It appeared he had been over a hundred miles away from Herrington at the time the crimes were committed. There was a stay of execution, and on 26 September, Wolfe was released from prison on a King's pardon. Meanwhile the members of the Society of Friends continued to look into the case for John Eden. Eventually, it was discovered that James Lincoln had given false evidence against the two men, no doubt to collect the reward that had been offered. Eden was also given a King's pardon and released.

On 4 August 1820 at the Durham Assizes, James Lincoln was tried and found guilty of wilful and corrupt perjury. In 1842, at the age of ninety, Lady Peat died with the true perpetrators of the crimes never being brought to justice.

A granddaughter of James Wolfe, Catherine Hindmarsh, when only nineteen was also murdered. One night in July 1846 she was seen in a public house having a drink with a strange man. The following morning her body was found on Lambton Railway line at the bottom of a steep drop. She had not been robbed as her purse was found nearby. Only Catherine and the perpetrator knew the motive for the murder. This also remains an unsolved crime.

Durham, 1816. Author's collection

Chapter 3

Insanity in the Family
1828

At Cowley House farm, which was near to Sedgefield, lived John Hutchinson, his two sons, Israel and Joseph, his daughter and her husband, Mr Lamb, and their children.

On a cold, winter's day, 10 November, the family sat down to their noon meal. The conversation at the table consisted of normal, everyday issues. Joseph, as was his usual routine, finished his meal first, left the table and went into the back kitchen. Without a word being spoken or any provocation, Joseph reappeared at the table with a large, iron poker in his hand. Before anyone had time to react, Joseph inflicted a heavy blow with the poker to his brother's head. Israel fell to the floor unconscious. Joseph then aimed the weapon at his brother-in-law but Lamb saw it coming and ducked. With just a slight graze to his forehead, he managed to hurriedly herd his wife and children out of harm's way. Joseph then turned on his father and beat him unmercifully. When his father was almost lifeless,

The Inn on the Green *at Sedgefield.* The author

Sedgefield Church and Lychgate. The author

Joseph went out of the house to get a hammer. Seemingly oblivious to the carnage he had wreaked, Joseph told a servant girl who had been in the yard during the attacks, to enter the house with him and have her dinner. He then re-entered the house and commenced beating his victims with the hammer. After several minutes of this frenzied attack, Joseph calmly went outside and regardless of the scene of slaughter he left behind he saddled a horse and rode to Durham.

As if nothing had taken place Joseph went to Mr Forsyth's

Newcastle Arms in South Elvet. This was the beerhouse the family used when they were in Durham. He left after a short while to return home. By this time the police had been alerted and were looking for him. Constable Crossling apprehended Joseph near Coxhoe. With the aid of two men who were passing in a gig, the constable managed to arrest and secure the murderer.

Joseph stood trial on 23 February 1829 on two counts of murder. Mr Oswald, a surgeon at Sedgefield Lunatic Asylum testified that the family had called him out to examine Joseph two years previously. At that time Mr Oswald had recommended that the family send him to an asylum, as he was not fit to be at large, but the family had ignored the recommendation. When Joseph was asked at the trial if he had anything to say, no sense could be made of his reply. Mr Frushard, governor of Durham gaol, his assistant, Mr Millbank and Mr Hepple, surgeon at the gaol, all testified they thought Joseph was of unsound mind. The jury brought in a verdict of guilty but insane and Justice Bailey sentenced Joseph to be detained at His Majesty's Pleasure.

Durham in the eighteenth century. Author's collection

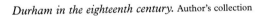

Chapter 4

Innocent or Guilty
1831

There can be no doubt that a murder was committed in August of 1830. The body was proof of that. Looking back through the records now, who committed the murder is perhaps not quite so clear. The man accused and found guilty protested his innocence until his final seconds.

Thomas Clarke and Mary Ann Westhorpe, both nineteen years of age, worked as servants for a family at Hallgarth water mill, near Pittington. On Sunday 8 August 1830 their master and mistress were away from home. Only those present in the house knew what actually took place during their employer's absence that afternoon. When the master and mistress returned it was to find Mary lying in a pool of blood and gore. Her skull had been bashed in and her throat cut. Clarke had made his way to Sherburn and the story that he told was that six men had entered the house and attacked them. No bruises or marks were found on

An eighteenth century water mill. Author's collection

Clarke's body and so he was presumed to be the guilty party.

Thomas Clarke's trial began on 25 February 1831 at 8 am before Justice Littledale. At ten that night the jury was sent to Mrs Best's *Half Moon Inn* with strict instructions not to discuss the case with anyone not concerned with the trial. Court was resumed the following morning and a little before one in the afternoon, the jury returned a verdict of guilty. Justice Littledale donned his black cap and asked Clarke why the harshest sentence should not be passed. Clarke replied 'I am innocent of the crime'. The judge then pronounced sentence of death on Clarke and added that his body should be given to the surgeons at Durham Infirmary for dissection. The sentence was carried out on the new drop in front of Durham courthouse on Monday, 28 February 1831. Just before the rope was placed around Clarke's neck he addressed the assembled crowd saying; 'Gentlemen I am innocent, I am going to suffer for another man's crime'.

The trial and execution caused a sensation and hundreds of people turned out to watch the demise of the unfortunate youth. Such was the publicity at the time that Mr Francis Humble of the *Durham Advertiser* composed a thirty-four-verse ballad relating to the events. Four of the verses were as follows:

At Hallgarth Mill near Pittington,
Was done a murder foul,
The female weak-the murderer strong,
No pity for her soul.

Her skull was broke, her throat was cut,
Her struggle soon was o'er;
And down she fell and fetch'd a sigh
And weltered in her gore.

Her fellow servant, Thomas Clarke,
To Sherburn slowly sped
And told a tale that stranger's six
Had done the dreadful deed

They've killed the lass, it was his tale,
And nearly have killed me,
But when upon him folks did look,
No bruises could they see.

Chapter 5

The Murder of a Magistrate
1832

Nicholas Fairles of South Shields was seventy-one years of age and a magistrate for the County of Durham. As such he was well thought of in the law-abiding community but would possibly have had many enemies amongst the pitmen and the criminal fraternity.

On 11 June at about five in the afternoon, Fairles was riding to Jarrow Colliery. Two pitmen suddenly appeared from nowhere on the pretence of asking for charity. As Fairles stopped his horse, one of the men took hold of his hand while the other dragged him from his horse. One hit the defenceless man on the head with a brick. Fairles was then kicked and beaten until he lost consciousness. The men ran off leaving their victim by the

Market Square, South Shields in the nineteenth century. Author's collection

Jarrow colliery in 1844 by T H Hair. Durham Mining Museum

roadside. A witness that had watched the assault from a nearby house quickly procured help. The unfortunate man lingered between life and death until 21 June but finally succumbed to his many injuries.

Important citizens, magistrates, clergy, the renowned historian Surtees and the Mayor of Newcastle, Archibald Reed, as well as family, were in attendance at Fairles' funeral.

The government and St Hilda's vestry each offered a reward of £100 for the apprehension and conviction of the men responsible for the murder. Because there had been witnesses it was not long before the police had the names of the men involved. One was Ralph Armstrong and the other William Jobling. The witnesses stated that it was Armstrong that had actually carried out the attack. He was never apprehended, probably because he took employment aboard a ship, but Jobling was soon arrested and sent for trial at the Durham Assizes on 1 August. He expressed his sorrow for his actions and stated that his meeting with Fairles was accidental and he had not meant to do anyone harm. He agreed that his sentence was just but denied having been the principal attacker during the assault.

The witness statements as to Jobling not actually being the murderer were ignored and he was found guilty of murder. Jobling's sentence was severe. He was to be hanged in front of the County

Port of Shields. Author's collection

Courts at Durham and his body to be then taken to nearby the scene of the murder and hung in chains on a gibbet. This was to be a deterrent to anyone contemplating such an act in the future.

Shortly after noon on 3 August, Jobling was led to the scaffold and the rope placed around his neck. As the last bolt was being withdrawn to open the drop, a person in the crowd shouted 'Farewell Jobling'. Jobling turned his head towards the voice and in doing so displaced the rope. As a result of this movement, Jobling was slowly strangled and his suffering continued for some minutes before he finally breathed his last. As was the custom, the body was left hanging for an hour before being cut down and

Sketch of William Jobling, from a woodcut by Mr Bouet. Author's collection

taken into the prison. Jobling's clothes were removed, his body covered in pitch and his clothes then replaced.

On Monday 6 August, at seven in the morning, the body was placed on a small four-wheeled wagon drawn by two horses. Officers of the gaol, the under sheriff, a troop of hussars and two groups of infantry, numbering about one hundred, accompanied the wagon on its route. They went by way of Chester-le-Street, Picktree, Sludge Row, Porto Bello, over the Black Fell to White Mare Pool then along the South Shields turnpike road to arrive at their destination of Jarrow Slake. Besides the escort the spectators numbered about 1,000. There perhaps would have been more, but there were not many pitmen present. They were, at that moment, holding a meeting on Boldon Fell:

The body was then lifted from the waggon. It was cased in flat bars of iron, the feet were placed in stirrups, from which a bar of iron went up each side of the head, and ended in a ring by which he was suspended; a bar from the collar went down the breast and another down the back; there were also bars on the inside of the legs, which communicated with the above; and cross bars at the ankles, the knees, the thighs, the bowels, the breast, the shoulders; the hands were hung by the sides and covered with pitch; the face was pitched and covered with a piece of white cloth.

The body was then placed on a handbarrow and taken to the gibbet. The gibbet had been erected at a spot within Jarrow Slake. At high tide the water would cover about five feet of the seventeen-foot high structure. Jobling's body was hoisted up and secured and, for a while, a police guard was on watch.

Sometime during the very dark night of 31 August, the body was removed by persons unknown and presumably buried in some secret location.

Chapter 6

Silence is Golden
1845

oseph Yates, a tailor, was having a drink in Barnard Castle with three other young men, George Barker, Thomas Routledge and John Brecken. As the evening progressed, Barker, Routledge and Brecken discovered that Yates had a fair amount of money on his person. The three then conspired to take the money from him. Later Yates paired off with a girl, Catherine Raine. Another local girl, Ann Humphreys, joined the other three men.

About midnight Yates and his lady friend were walking along the banks of the Tees unaware that his three drinking companions and Ann Humphreys were following. Barker, Routledge and Brecken attacked Yates, and after taking his money, threw him into the swollen Tees. On returning to the town over the bridge, the three men threatened the girls that they would take vengeance on them if they spoke of what had

Barnard Castle in the eighteenth century. Author's collection

The River Tees at Barnard Castle. The author

taken place. Catherine Raine refused to say she would be silent so she was also thrown into the river to drown. The bodies were discovered a few days later and although the three men involved and Humphreys were suspected and questioned, nothing could be proved.

Humphreys' conscience must have bothered her because a year later she reported what had happened to the authorities. The men were acquitted at the York Assizes in August 1846 because the girl's testimony was unsupported. The matter was, however, looked into further and evidence was procured to corroborate Humphreys' testimony. The three men were then arraigned for the robbery only. At York Assizes on 16 March 1847 they were sentenced to fifteen years transportation. His Lordship expressed regrets that they had escaped the charge of murder. The two trials cost the County of York £1,500, an enormous sum of money at that time.

York Assizes in 1895. Author's collection

Chapter 7

Raby Castle
1848-49

On 2 February, John Shirley, who was head gamekeeper and whipper-in to the Duke of Cleveland was shot by a party of poachers. An affray took place near Raby Castle. After the shooting the poachers beat Shirley so severely, he later died of his injuries. Two men, William Thompson and William Dowson were convicted of the crime before Baron Alderson at Durham on 8 March. Dowson was transported for life. Thompson was executed on 25 March. A detachment of the 7th (Black Horse) Dragoons were on duty at the execution.

On 21 January 1849 another of the Duke of Cleveland's gamekeepers, a man by the name of May, was murdered at Toundle Myers, near West Auckland. Like Shirley, May had been shot. The bullet had gone into the back of his head.

The south-west aspect of Raby Castle in 1784. Author's collection

Raby Castle in 2003. Author's collection

May had given evidence at the Durham Assizes relating to Shirley's murder against Thompson and Dowson. It was, therefore, assumed that he had been shot by some of the convicted men's friends. Three men, Neasham, Simpson and Peverly, were apprehended after mutually incriminating each other. On 28 July Neasham was tried for May's murder before Justice Pattison. Simpson and Peverly gave evidence against Neasham but he was acquitted.

Chapter 8

The Stolen Infant
1854

Mary Thompson lived with her husband, Richard, and their thirteen-month old infant, Margaret Ann, in Minorca Place at the east end of Sunderland. In June of 1853 Mary was confined to bed through illness. A young woman, who said her name was Isabella Grozier, knocked on her door and asked if she could attend to her. Mary, because she was quite helpless at the time, took the woman into her service offering to pay her 2s (10p) a week to take care of her and little Margaret.

On 17 June Mary saw Isabella removing some of Margaret's clothes from the drawer in which they were kept. When asked what she was doing Isabella replied 'nothing'. Mary was, at that time, quite ill, so did not pursue her questioning.

On 18 June at about eight in the morning Isabella went an errand for Mary taking the child with her. They had not returned when Mary's husband, Richard, came home from work at noon that day. He immediately informed the police. The town of Sunderland was searched all that day and throughout the night, but with no trace of the woman and the little girl. The police had handbills made and circulated extensively throughout the town and surrounding areas

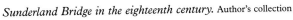

Sunderland Bridge in the eighteenth century. Author's collection

offering a £5 reward and giving a description of the child and the woman she was with. The woman was described as having a gypsy-like appearance with a very dark complexion, black, closely cropped hair, of medium build and aged about twenty-five. Although strenuous efforts were continued by the police to find the pair they seemed to have vanished. Summer drifted into winter with no sign of Margaret or the mysterious woman.

On 2 January 1854 a woman was admitted into the workhouse at Bishop Auckland. She had a little girl with her and both were covered in vermin and in a filthy state. The woman gave her name as Isabella Mood and said she was married to a stonemason from Hartlepool, Richard, and that the child, Margaret Ann, was theirs. The little girl had a black eye and some bruising on her back, which the woman said was because she had fallen the night before. They were sent to the probationary ward where the medical officer for the workhouse, Valentine Hutchinson, examined them both. When he asked how the child had come to have the injuries, Isabella changed her story saying that her name was Thompson and that her husband had beaten the child. Dr Hutchinson saw no other sign of illness. Ann Harrison, an inmate of the workhouse, washed the little girl and saw that she and Isabella were comfortable. Two nights later Isabella sent for Ann saying that

Market Place and Town Hall, Bishop Auckland. Author's collection

the child was in a fit. When Ann arrived she could see the child was in distress and so sent for Dr Hutchinson. He prescribed a warm bath and cod liver oil, which was the usual remedy for fits. This was done and the child revived, she was then put to bed with Isabella with a fire in the room. At eleven the following night the doctor was sent for again. He saw a cut on the forehead and a bruise on the left side of the Margaret's head. Isabella told him that the child had hit herself on the iron bedpost during a fit. This time the doctor ordered that Isabella and Margaret were not to be left alone. Ann sat with them until after midnight. Isabella then told Ann that the child seemed to be improving so there was no need for her to stay with them any longer. Ann left them and went to her own bed. The following morning she looked in to the room and with Margaret sitting on her knee, Isabella told Ann the little girl was much better. Shortly afterwards Mary Duckworth, the cook at the workhouse, looked in and seeing Margaret still on Isabella's knee, went to have a closer look. A handkerchief was over the little girl's face and when Mary removed it she saw Margaret was dead. Mary told Isabella to lay the child down. Isabella threw the lifeless little body onto the bed. Mary called Ann who washed the body of the little girl. As was the usual routine, after seeing to that necessary task, Ann proceeded to clean the room and noticed spots of blood on the corner of the stone mantelpiece and on the fireside. Looking around she saw more blood on the floorboards and some on the wall. Ann informed the master of the workhouse, Thomas Reynolds, who called in the police and Isabella was taken into custody. Dr Hutchinson immediately performed a postmortem on the small body. As well as the two injuries he had seen previously he found other bruises on different parts of the body. There were also three fractures to the skull, one of which had been the cause of death. The fracture had detached part of the bone of the skull and in the doctor's opinion all the injuries had been caused with extreme violence, probably with a blunt instrument. On inspection of the mantelpiece it was found there was a dent that corresponded to the mark on Margaret's skull. In Dr Hutchinson's opinion, the child had been brutally murdered by being swung against the mantelpiece again and again until lifeless.

The body of the little girl was buried and the police began to question Isabella. They then realised that she matched the description of the woman who had abducted a little girl in Sunderland seven months previously. Also, at the workhouse, she had given the child's name as Margaret Ann Thompson, which was the name of the little girl that was taken. Mary and Richard Thompson were brought to Bishop Auckland by Inspector Temple and after repeating their story to the coroner he ordered the small body to be disinterred. When the sexton at South Church showed them the body, the distraught parents immediately identified it as their missing daughter. Mr and Mrs Thompson then went to Durham gaol and Mary Thompson identified the prisoner being held there as Isabella Grozier, the woman who had disappeared with baby Margaret.

A complicated story emerged at the ensuing Durham Assizes. The probationary ward where Isabella and Margaret had been staying, although not locked inside, was locked to the outside world. No one could have entered or left without a key.

The jury was instructed that Margaret Ann Thompson had without a doubt, been murdered by Isabella. They now had the unenviable task of deciding whether her death was carried out with malice aforethought. In which case it would be wilful murder and the perpetrator would be executed, or whether Isabella Grozier was insane and could then not be held responsible for her actions.

Many of Mary and Richard's Thompson's neighbours came forward to say that they recognised the prisoner as the woman

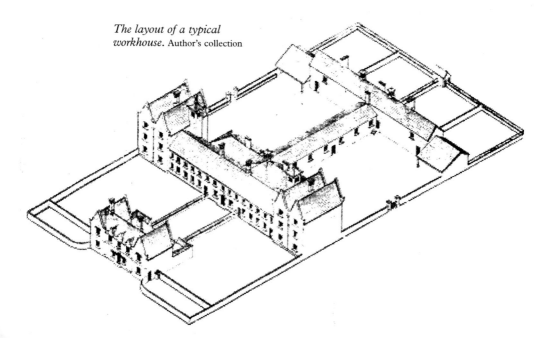

The layout of a typical workhouse. Author's collection

who had worked in the Thompson's house and that they had seen her with little Margaret on the morning she was abducted. As well as having the child with her she was also carrying a bundle.

One of the first witnesses was Elizabeth Willis who kept a lodging house. She stated that Isabella, the little girl and a man calling himself John Thompson had stayed at her house for just over a week in December 1853. The second night they were at the house the man, who Elizabeth now knew to be John Mood not Thompson, had slapped the child across the back with great violence. Isabella had flung the child at Elizabeth when the landlady tried to remonstrate with the man about his act.

Isabella's statement was:

I am the wife of Robert Thompson. I left him at Hartlepool in June last. He is a stonemason. The deceased Margaret Ann Thompson is his child. I have since I left my husband been cohabitating with John Mood who is now here. I left Willis' lodging house on the Wednesday before the New Year with Mood. We were in the gas house that night. I was after at Mrs MacIntyre's. Mood left me to seek work. I found him at the Black Boy Tile Sheds. He said it was too cold he could not stand work. I remained there with him on Saturday and Sunday nights. I came to the workhouse on Monday. He said he was going to Crook. I have not seen him again until this morning. I did not cause the death of the child from any blow whatsoever. I might fling her down many a time, but never gave her a blow as described. I did not fling her at Mrs Willis as she stated. I did not do so here. She took a fit on Wednesday night. It was some time before I went for assistance. She has taken fits since she was three months old.

John Mood said that Margaret had sustained the black eye when Isabella had slipped and fell with the child in her arms.

Isabella's family had lived in Sunderland where she had been brought up with her brother, James. Her father had been a master mariner so was away at sea more than at home. She and her brother, who was now also a master mariner, had a good education. Her brother stated that Isabella had always been a little 'queer'. She would talk to herself and make dolls from bits of rag and caress them as if they were living children. The family thought that Isabella would grow out of her strange ways but as she became older she got worse.

About fourteen months before these events took place, Isabella had stayed at the House of Refuge in Sunderland. A woman named Hannah Wilkinson had stayed there at the same time and had slept in the same room as Isabella. Hannah said that Isabella did not seem to be of sound mind as she mumbled and talked to herself and had once tried to cut her own throat. Mr Davidson from the House of Refuge stated that Isabella had told him that she had a child to a man named Cormack from Hartlepool. One of the wardens at Durham gaol, Jane Summerville, said that Isabella 'conducted herself in a peculiar manner'. Another warden and the prison doctor thought Isabella quite sane.

As to why Isabella had taken the child in the first place, the explanation from the prosecution was, that if you were a beggar, people were more charitable towards a person with a child. Isabella's defence, Mr Stack, in his final argument asked if the child had been Isabella's bread and butter, why then would she kill her? Directing his words to the jury he said:

> The evidence upon which you shall come to a verdict, whatever it may be, is one of a purely circumstantial character; there is nothing direct about it, the eye of man hath not seen, nor hath the tongue of eye witness told to another who committed this murder. Before now wrongful verdicts have been given upon such testimony and your innocent fellow-creatures have been sent to their graves.

The jury was a long time deliberating on the case but eventually returned a verdict of guilty but insane. Isabella Thompson was sentenced to be detained at Her Majesty's Pleasure.

High Street in East Sunderland. Author's collection

Chapter 9

Highway Robbery
1855

Robert Stirling was twenty-six when he moved to Burnopfield and became an assistant to a surgeon, Mr Watson. The young man was said by the most eminent in his profession to be very amiable and to have considerable talent. Stirling had only been in the neighbourhood and his new employment for ten days when on 1 November he was sent to visit patients at The Spen and Thornley. It was assumed by Mr Watson that Stirling had been delayed in a professional capacity when he did not return that evening. The following morning when there was still no sign of Stirling, panic bells began to ring. Watson sent a junior assistant to make enquiries. It was ascertained that, on Friday, two men had been seen going towards Newcastle in a gig and one may have been Stirling. It was assumed he had accepted a lift and had decided to visit Newcastle town. A few days then elapsed and Watson became worried again and contacted Stirling's father who lived in Kirkintolloch in Scotland. As soon as Mr Stirling arrived in the village he immediately organised a search party to look for his son. His father found Robert Stirling's body on the morning of 6 November hidden in undergrowth in Smaile's Wood near Derwent Bridge.

Enquiries led to a reconstruction of what had taken place. Stirling had completed his visits and at around two o'clock in the afternoon had walked down Smaile's Lane to reach the road to Burnopfield. As he came to an angle in the road someone shot him from behind the hedge. The bullet entered his right groin. The perpetrator had then struck his victim in the face and head with the butt end of the gun and cut his throat. Stirling's body had then been dragged by the feet over the hedge and left in undergrowth. His purse, ring, watch and 18s (90p) in silver from his pocket had been taken. The watch was very distinctive. It was silver in a glass case. The figures were Roman numerals and a wreath surrounded the dial.

John Bowes owned extensive estates and land in the area. The day the murder was committed was rent day at Gibside. It was possible that the murderer assumed Stirling to be a tenant of John Bowes and if on his way to pay his rent, would be carrying a considerable amount of money. If this was so, then the murderer was no stranger to the area.

The police were at a loss as to where to begin to look. Then, a few days after the crime, some boys were at the place the crime was committed, looking for trophies no doubt! One of the boys, Samuel Bennet, was disturbing some leaves with a branch when something caught his eye. It was a glass button, unusual because it had a copper shank. The boy took it to the police. Then a cattle dealer, Joseph Stobart, came forward with information. He had been walking down the lane that fateful day when he came upon two men. A little further on he passed another man whom he spoke to. The man replied with a Scottish accent so this must have been Stirling. A few minutes later, as Stobart had turned a corner in the lane he heard a gunshot. Nothing was thought about it at the time because there were often sportsmen in that area shooting birds. Other witnesses reported seeing a suspicious looking man lurking about the neighbourhood.

The police traced a man to Glasgow and he was arrested. On his person was found a bloodstained handkerchief. Suspicion also fell on two other local men and they were subsequently arrested. Richard Rayne, a blacksmith and John Cain. Both were known poachers and carried guns. The first man was released, as there was no evidence against him. At an inquest heard on 3 January 1856, an additional witness came forward. He swore that the two men that were under arrest, at the time and on the day of the murder, had been walking in South Shield Row towards Durham so could not have killed Stirling.

Rayne and Cain were arraigned at Durham Assizes on 6 March 1856 before Baron Martin. Stobart was asked if Cain and Rayne were the men he saw in the lane. He said he could not swear to it but they looked similar to the men he had seen. The police went to a house in Newcastle where one of the men lived and seized his clothes. Among the clothes was a waistcoat with buttons similar to the one found in the undergrowth. The

Old houses in Newcastle. Author's collection

fourth button on the waistcoat was missing. The other three remaining buttons were scratched. It was also ascertained that a man fitting Rayne's description had pawned a watch the day after the murder was committed. This was the only evidence that the police had. Baron Martin remanded the men to the Summer Assizes because the evidence against them was incomplete.

The two men were tried on 25 and 26 July before Justice Willes. A variety of conflicting circumstantial evidence was bandied back and forward during the trial and at the end of the two days a verdict of not guilty was returned.

No one else was ever arrested for the murder and it remains unsolved to this day.

Chapter 10

Victims of Jealousy

Jarrow, 1859

Dorothy Wilthew had borne her husband, John Shaftoe, eleven children. They had lived at Hebburn in Drewitt's buildings near Jarrow railway station for about two years. As well as several of their children living with them, to supplement a meagre income, there was also a lodger, a man by the name of George Charlton. Wilthew was known as a violent man who often abused his wife, especially when he had been drinking. He had been seen hitting and kicking her, and, on more than one occasion had been heard threatening to cut her throat.

On Monday 18 July Charlton and Wilthew left Palmer's shipbuilding yard, where they both worked, at six o'clock and walked home together as usual. The pair sat in Wilthew's house and talked about general things. Charlton went to bed at about eleven that night leaving Wilthew eating his supper and Dorothy working around the house. Neither of the men had a drink at all that evening. At about four the following morning Charlton was awoken by someone entering his room. When he roused himself and looked up, Dorothy was standing at the side of his bed. She

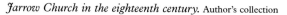

Jarrow Church in the eighteenth century. Author's collection

Palmer's shipbuilding works near Jarrow. Author's collection

had her hand to her throat and blood was dripping down her nightdress and forming a pool on the floor. Dorothy, unable to speak, beckoned Charlton to look at the passage outside his room that led to the privy. Wilthew, dressed in his shirt and trousers, was walking down the passage. Charlton stopped him and asked what he had done but Wilthew did not reply. Charlton then shouted for help and some neighbours arrived to assist, but it was too late. Dorothy died a few minutes later from the terrible gash to her throat. The deep cut had been inflicted with a razor. While the neighbours and a doctor attended to the dead woman, Charlton went to find Wilthew. He was lying in his bedroom with a self-inflicted cut to his own throat. Although the cut was deep it was in no way a threat on Wilthew's life and a doctor was able to stitch the wound.

Wilthew was arrested and stood trial for his wife's murder. The jury was made up of Isaac Johnson and James Hardy of Gateshead, George Coltman, James Groves and James Armstrong of Hartlepool, John Anderson and John Campbell of Bishopwearmouth, Sheraton Brown of Elwick, Christopher Jackson of Darlington, Henry Althorp of Benning, John Humphrey of Norton and Henry Angus of Bagnail.

Through witness's statements it transpired that Wilthew had told a neighbour and one of his daughters that he was going to cut Dorothy's throat because he was jealous of her. When all the evidence had been submitted the jury agreed that the murder was premeditated and that Wilthew was of sound mind.

Justice Keating donned his black cap and said:

John Shaftoe Wilthew, you have been convicted of the crime of murder, that murder upon your own wife, the mother of eleven

Elvet Bridge in Durham. Author's collection

*children and for many years your partner in life, and you have
done it under an unfounded suspicion of the infidelity of your
wife. You have all the appearance of a person perfectly sane,
perfectly conscious of his acts. You have indeed committed a great
and heinous offence.*

He then went on to pronounce sentence of death on Wilthew.

On 11 August 1859 Askern the executioner hanged Wilthew
on the drop on the Assize Court's green in Old Elvet in Durham.
As Wilthew died, the stitches in the wound in his neck gave way
and a large gaping wound was displayed to the watching crowds.

Urpeth: 1860

Milner Lockey, his wife, Elizabeth, and her three children from
a previous marriage, had moved to a cottage at Urpeth Mill
from Urpeth Colliery. Lockey was sixty years of age and
Elizabeth was forty-nine. Lockey also had a son and daughter,
now grown, from a previous marriage. Urpeth Mill house was
occupied by a miller named Mr T C Bell. The cottage was next
door to the mill house and consisted of just two rooms, one
downstairs and one upstairs. After a short while Lockey and his
wife separated. Lockey moved out and Elizabeth and her
children continued to reside at the cottage. Just after the
Lockey's separation Bell, the miller went into bankruptcy and
had to leave the mill house.

Thomas Harrison had been a member of the police force but
had been forced to resign because he had lost the use of one eye.

He took employment as messenger's bailiff for the Bankruptcy Court and as such he was put in possession of Bell's effects. Harrison resided in the mill house until the furniture and effects were disposed of. He then went to lodge at the cottage with Elizabeth until the crops could be harvested and sold. Harrison slept in a bed in the downstairs room and Elizabeth and her children slept upstairs on a mattress on the floor.

On 29 November, in the downstairs room of the cottage, Milner Lockey attacked his wife and Harrison with a knife. Elizabeth, although severely wounded, survived, but Harrison died instantly from his wounds.

At his trial before Justice Keating, Lockey gave his version of the events that had taken place prior to and during the attack he had carried out. He said he had gone to visit his wife and she had not been very pleasant to him. Harrison was there and would not go to bed so the three of them had sat up until about eleven at night. Eventually, Elizabeth said she was going upstairs so Lockey had followed her. He had lain down on the floor beside the mattress that his wife and the children slept on. After about an hour Lockey had become cold and asked if he could sleep on the mattress. He had said to his wife that it was not fair that another man should have a bed to sleep on while he had to sleep on the floor after coming nineteen miles to visit her. Lockey had then told his wife that he could pay for a bed as he had a sovereign, (£1). Elizabeth then rose from the mattress and went downstairs leaving Lockey sleeping with the children for the remainder of the night.

On the following morning Elizabeth gave him coffee and while he was drinking it her conversation was all about Harrison. As Lockey was leaving the cottage Elizabeth asked him for the sovereign. He told her she could have it if he could move back in with her. Elizabeth had said she would think about it. Lockey then went to stay with his son until Monday morning and then went to work. About a week later Lockey received a letter from his daughter, Dorothy:

Brecondykes, Sept. 23, 1860.

Dear Father This comes with my kind love to you, hoping to find you well, as it leaves me at present, thank God for it. I write to inform you that your wife has been busy at Brecondykes and laid you out for everything that was bad-that you offered her a sovereign if she would let you come back and live with her again, and she told you that she would not. She was at Pelton that day that you went away, and was as drunk as a pig. If you will take my advice you will never come where she is again, till you are forced to it; but you can please yourself because everyone is talking about what a fool you are. Last time she was at Brecondyke she told them that you had been saying what a fool you were to marry such a woman; that you said she was living with another man; and that she threw a glass of ale at you; and what a fool she was for not putting such a man as you into gaol, as you were such a bad un. It is only your money she wants, and to do as she likes.

When Lockey read the letter it made him angry, especially as he felt Elizabeth had not treated him well when he last visited her. He decided to go to the cottage and speak to his wife.

On 29 November he opened the door of the cottage. Lockey said that what he saw sent him into an uncontrollable rage. Elizabeth and Thomas Harrison were lying together on the bed. Elizabeth jumped from the bed and Lockey said to her 'Well hinny how art thou' she answered 'middling' to which he replied, 'I think you are going on bonny here; damn your blood I've a good mind to kill you both'. He then pulled a knife from his pocket and stabbed Elizabeth and then Harrison.

Elizabeth Lockey, although still very weak from her injury, attended the trial as a witness. She admitted asking for the sovereign but denied that she had told her husband that she would think about him moving back in with her.

It was well known that Lockey wanted to move back in with his wife and that he was very jealous of her. Robert Coulson, a pitman now at Coundon, had worked with Lockey at Leasingthorne Colliery. Coulson stated that Lockey was jealous, first of the miller and then Harrison and had often spoken threats against his wife. Lockey had also said that if his wife would not live with him then she would live with no one else.

Another witness was Francis Oughton who had known Lockey for some years. Early on the day the crime was committed, Oughton had bumped into Lockey as he was leaving Durham and had invited him to go for a drink at his house in

Claypath in Durham during the nineteenth century. Author's collection

Pity Me. While they were having a drink, Lockey had told Oughton that he was on his way to Urpeth Mill. He then said,

> *There is jealousy, and if that one-eyed b..... is there, I'll put an end to them both. I won't be hanged for them for I'll put an end to my own existence after that.*

Oughton said that at the time Lockey had a spring-backed knife in his possession. The next witness was Samuel, one of Elizabeth's sons. The young boy stated that on the night in question Harrison had gone to bed early, complaining of feeling poorly. Samuel had gone to bed just afterwards but was still awake when he heard his mother and Lockey shouting angrily at each other. Lockey was swearing at Elizabeth so Samuel got out of bed and went downstairs. Lockey was sitting on a table by the window. Samuel's clothes were on a stool beside the table. As the boy was putting his clothes on he saw that Lockey had a knife. The next minute the knife was opened and Lockey lunged at Elizabeth stabbing her in the thigh. Elizabeth was fully dressed and when she lifted her long skirt, Samuel saw blood streaming down her leg. At this, Harrison, who was still on his bed shouted to Lockey to stop. Lockey swung around and savagely attacked Harrison driving the knife in deeper and deeper. Blood was all over the bed and streaming onto the floor. Elizabeth managed to gather her wits and wrestle the knife from her husband's hand while at the same time motioning Samuel to go for help. The boy went to the Ridings, a place about half a mile away, and told a neighbour, Edward Hart, what had happened. Hart followed Samuel back to the cottage to find both Mr and Mrs Lockey standing at the door. Elizabeth told Hart to go inside because her husband had murdered a man. Lockey shouted that it was nonsense and the woman was off her head. Elizabeth then ran from the cottage with her husband in pursuit. On Hart entering the cottage he found Harrison slumped in a chair covered in blood. He was dead. Elizabeth went to notify the police and they searched the area around the cottage. Lockey was found hiding in a pig-sty. He made no comment when charged with Harrison's murder. There were no marks of violence found on the prisoner to indicate that he had been in a struggle. A small clasp knife was found in his pocket. Elizabeth's clothes were examined and the cuts in the material from the knife proved that she had been fully dressed at the time of the attack.

A man named Forster owned an ironmonger's shop in Durham. He told the police that a man strongly resembling Lockey had bought a knife from him on the morning of the day that the crime took place. Forster said that the man had been specific in the type of knife he wished to purchase. The knife used to kill Harrison was produced and Forster identified it as having come from his shop. The knife was spring-backed with a four-inch blade and made a very formidable weapon. Oughton also identified the knife as the one Lockey was carrying when he met him on the road out of Durham.

Justice Keating instructed the jury that Lockey had admitted to the attacks but they must decide whether he should be found guilty of murder or manslaughter. If they thought that the crime had been in a fit of passion because Elizabeth had been caught in a compromising situation, then the verdict would be manslaughter. If, however, Lockey had gone to the cottage with felonious intent then the verdict must be murder.

The jury decided that Lockey had lied about his wife being in bed with Harrison as it was proven that she had been fully dressed during the attack. Also as Lockey already had a small knife for everyday use why would he wish to purchase a large brand new

Framwellgate Bridge in Durham, 1904. Author's collection

one unless his intent was to use it in the way that he did. Lockey was fifty-eight and a man of great physical strength and very fit. The jury felt that Harrison had not stood a chance against Lockey's strength and violent jealous rage. They found the prisoner guilty of murder with no recommendation for mercy.

Thomas Askern carried out Lockey's execution on 27 December 1860.

Sunderland: 1868

John Dolan was a thirty-seven year old Irish labourer. He lived with Catherine Keeshan who had a lodging house at 49 Union Lane in Sunderland. Another two men, Edward Collins and Hugh John Ward also resided in the house as lodgers. Ward had only been living in the house for about five weeks and at first it seemed that he and Dolan were on friendly terms. On 8 December the two men went for a walk and stopped off somewhere and had a drink. It was thought later that there must have been some conversation relating to Catherine, Dolan's paramour. When the two men returned to the house Dolan gave Catherine money to buy some ale. When she returned with the quart of alcohol, Ward helped himself to a glass and then offered one to Dolan. Dolan refused, saying he had to be up for work in the morning. Ward said there was too much for him to drink by himself so Dolan accepted a glass. Ward then handed a glass to Catherine, which she accepted. At

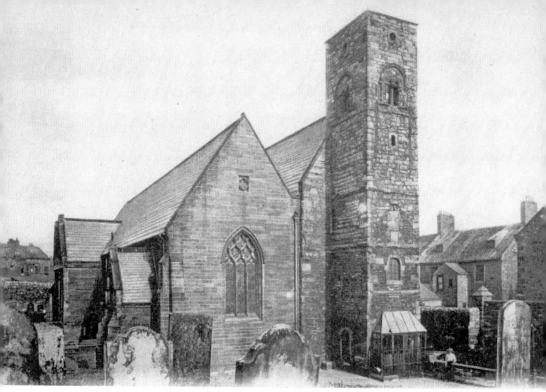

Monkwearmouth Parish Church in Sunderland. Author's collection

this Dolan jumped up in a jealous rage. He seized Catherine by the hair and dragged her to the bedroom and viciously bit her breast. Catherine shouted for Ward to help her. When Ward went to assist, Dolan told him it was okay, he was not going to do Catherine any harm, so Ward went and sat down in the kitchen. Dolan then started again on Catherine and she screamed for help. Ward and Dolan then started to fight and Catherine ran for police assistance. When a police constable arrived he calmed the situation but as he had not witnessed the affray he would not make an arrest. Catherine pleaded with him to take Dolan as she thought there would be 'murder done' if he was left in the house, but to no avail. As soon as the constable was gone Dolan emerged from the bedroom with a knife. Catherine jumped out of a window and ran down the street screaming 'murder'.

The other man staying in the house, Collins, had by now awoken. As he came out of his room to see what was going on he saw Dolan go up to Ward, who was sitting near the fireplace. Dolan had a shoemaker's knife in his hand and before Ward knew what was happening Dolan lunged at him.

The first thrust of the knife disemboweled his victim; the second thrust took out his left eye. Collins managed to grab Dolan and hold him until Catherine arrived with the police a few seconds later.

Dolan was tried at Durham Assizes before Justice Lush and was found guilty of murder and sentenced to death. The prisoner started shouting that it was not his fault and that the witnesses had sworn his life away and that he had been found guilty because he had bad counsel. Justice Lush said that Dolan had had good counsel and there had been no extenuating circumstances for the cold blooded, brutal murder that he had carried out. William Calcraft hanged Dolan on 22 March 1869. John McConville was hanged for a murder at

William Calcraft, executioner from 1829-74. Author's collection

Darlington at the same time. These were the first private executions to take place at Durham.

Durham: 1873

Jane Johnson was born at Urpeth, where her father, Edward Johnson, worked as a miner. The family later moved to Annfield Plain and Jane eventually married. Her husband, Henry Atchison, came from Greencroft's Cottages near Lanchester. Her marriage was not a happy one and the couple parted. By this time she had a child. Jane went to stay with relatives at Felling, near Newcastle. Whilst living there she met William Thompson. When they decided to marry there were strong objections from Jane's family because the marriage would be illegal as she and Atchinson had never been divorced. Jane disputed the family's misgivings because she believed that her husband, who was living at Howden, near Crook, had taken himself another wife. Jane, who was twenty by this time, married William Thompson at Gateshead Registry Office in February of 1872.

This second marriage turned out no better than the first and

Front Street, Lancaster in the early twentieth century. Durham Federation of Women's Institutes and Countryside Books.

eventually Jane left her husband and went to live with her father at Pontop Cottages. Although her father had been strongly opposed to this union and had not spoken to his daughter from the time she married, he welcomed Jane into his house in her time of need. It was not long before Thompson followed his wife and promised to treat her 'more kindly' in future. Jane's father decided to give Thompson a chance and allowed him to stay.

The couple, according to Jane's father, lived in harmony for about six weeks until Saturday, 4 October 1873. Thompson, his wife and her father went to Newcastle for the day. On their return

High Street in Gateshead, 1910. Author's collection

The Old Nag's Head *in Newcastle during the nineteenth century.* Author's collection

Jane started to prepare the supper. While she was doing this, she asked her father to go and buy some beer. Johnson, as he thought, left the couple in seemingly good spirits and speaking kindly to each other. The public house was not far from where they lived. Johnson had just given his order for the beer when a young girl rushed in and shouted to him to come quickly as his daughter was lying dead on the floor of a neighbour's house.

It transpired that while the family was returning from Newcastle they had travelled back on Mr Bone's brake with two women from Annfield Plain. Ann Grace Watson, the wife of a blacksmith at South Derwent Colliery, was sitting between Jane and her husband and told of the events that took place. Thompson had slapped Jane across the face and accused her of fancying a man she had spoken to in Newcastle. He had then said 'Wait until we get home. It will be either you or me for it'. Jane had replied:

> *It will be either you or me for it. You are not going to murder me. You always commence to abuse me when my father goes out.*

Sarah Graham, the wife of a mason, said that when the brake reached Pelton Bank, Thompson alighted and walked up the bank. Sarah asked Jane if he was her husband. Jane had answered that he was and was jealous because she had been talking to her cousin in Newcastle. Thompson then returned to the brake and on reaching Oxhill, had asked Jane for money. Jane refused and Thompson again threatened her saying 'I will be alright with you when we get home'. As they reached Annfield Plain, Thompson struck Jane in the face, she returned the blow then began to cry.

That same evening, Mary Ann Parker, a neighbour who lived two doors up from Johnson's house, heard a scream. Jane Thompson entered Mary's house a few seconds later bleeding profusely from a wound to her throat. Mary and another neighbour, Ann Scullan, went to Jane's assistance but she died a few minutes later. Elizabeth Parker, who was nine and Mary Ann Hall were in the road at the time and had seen William Thompson running away. The police were called and they immediately went to search for Thompson. He was arrested at his brother's house at Dipton.

Thompson's story was, that when they were at Newcastle they had gone into a public house to eat. Some

A cut-throat razor. The author

men were there that Jane knew and she went off with them leaving Thompson sitting by himself 'like a child'. When the family returned home and Johnson had gone to buy the beer, the couple had had words about Jane's behavior. Thompson said he had put his arms on the table and placed his head in them and when he looked up Jane had a razor in her hand. Thompson stood up and as Jane ran to the door, he followed and struck her. Jane then cut her own throat. The medical evidence proved otherwise. John Gilland Hunter, a surgeon, performed a post-mortem on the body. His findings were that the cut had been made from behind, probably with a razor, and was so deep the head was nearly severed from the body. Only the vertebrae were keeping the head attached to the body.

William Thompson was sent to trial at the Durham Assizes before Justice Honeyman and was found guilty of the wilful murder of his wife. He was assisted to meet his maker by the executioner, William Marwood, on 5 January 1874. Two others, Charles Dawson and Edward Gough, were also hanged for murder at Durham on that same morning.

Hetton: 1891
John William Johnson had lived with and worked for Margaret Addison for about eighteen years. Margaret had a farmhouse at Four Lane Ends in Hetton and Johnson did the odd jobs about the place. Johnson's drinking habits had become worse over the past year and eventually Margaret threw him out. Margaret, who was fifty-two years old, had become involved with a man named Andrew Simpson and was to marry him.

After his eviction from the farmhouse Johnson began telling anyone who would listen that he would never allow Margaret to marry another man. He was often seen loitering around the farmhouse seemingly watching for his lost mistress.

On Saturday morning, 30 October, Margaret was on her way to Hetton Station to take the train to Spennymoor to visit her mother. She had just reached the end of Springwell Terrace, near to the weekend entrance of the station, when Johnson approached her. A little girl, Sarah Ellen McCormack and a labourer, William Walker, witnessed what happened next. Johnson nodded civilly to Walker as he passed him and then went up to Margaret and tapped her on the shoulder and said something to her. He then walked a few feet away from her, turned with his hands behind his back and without speaking a word he produced a revolver and fired two shots in rapid succession. One shot penetrated Margaret's temple, the other her brow. She fell to the ground having been killed instantly. Johnson, still without speaking, then turned away and walked towards the nearby police station.

Sarah Cartwright, the wife of the police sergeant was in the kitchen to the front of the police station when Johnson walked in. Imagine her astonishment when he told her he had 'murdered the landlady.' Mrs Cartwright took him to a cell and locked him in. She then asked him to empty his pockets. Johnson handed her the revolver, which was still warm, three cartridges, a knife and a bunch of keys.

That same night, Johnson was taken before Mr F Stobbart JP of Biddick Hall, Houghton-le-Spring, who remanded him into custody. Mr Graham the Coroner for the Easington Ward held the initial inquest at the New Inn in Four Lane Ends at Hetton. He was found guilty of murder and committed for trial to the Durham Assizes.

Johnson pleaded guilty and chose not to be defended at the trial. The jury found him guilty of murder. Before pronouncing sentence of death, Justice Wills made a closing statement. He spoke of his abhorrence of the taking of a woman's life for no more reason than jealousy because the woman was to marry another. Johnson presented a written statement to Justice Wills asking that it be given to the press. When the press asked to read the statement they were refused permission and were told they would have to apply to the Secretary of the State. The sentence of death on John William Johnson was carried out on 22 December 1891 within the walls of Durham gaol by the executioner James Billington.

Hetton colliery in 1844 by T H Hair. Durham Mining Museum

Chapter 11

An Incestuous Relationship
1860

Until 1835, when a new colliery was established about a mile to the south, the village of Cornforth was agricultural. To accommodate the workers a new village sprang up and was known as West Cornforth.

On Thursday, 23 August of 1860, West Cornforth was rocked by the events that took place. A young woman and her newborn baby had died under very suspicious circumstances.

The village was a tight-knit community that never locked their doors against one another. But, prior to that fateful Thursday, rumour and suspicion had been rife amongst the inhabitants that something was amiss. The reason for this was that at the house of Robert Simpson the doors had been closed for several days and there was mention that his daughter was pregnant.

Simpson was a cartman who had previously been an innkeeper in Darlington. His daughter, Jane, was twenty-two and unmarried. In 1858 she had formed a relationship with a man named Hugh Devon. They were to be married, but for some reason that was not common knowledge, Hugh had called the relationship off. In about March of 1860 he had moved away from the area. Jane had a child of about two years old but it was not certain whether Hugh had been the father. Local gossip pointed to an incestuous relationship between father and daughter.

Towards the end of June, Jane had gone to a neighbour, Margaret Foulkes, asking for some bread. She told Margaret that she had had nothing to eat since the previous day and was hungry and felt very poorly. Margaret suspected that Jane was pregnant but on asking her, Jane at first denied it. Eventually admitting that she was, Jane started to cry saying that her father did not know and she had no clothes for a baby. Margaret promised to help Jane when her time came, but did not ask

Northgate in Darlington, 1905. Author's collection

when that was. A few days later Margaret told Simpson that his daughter was pregnant but he would not believe her. One of the village women, Jane Thompson, had also suspected that Jane was pregnant, but had not mentioned it to anyone.

On Tuesday, 14 August, a neighbour, Mary Rutherford, who knew Jane well, called in to see her. Jane was sitting by the fire and was mumbling incoherently. Mary was so alarmed at Jane's appearance that she went to call for another woman, Ann Heavisides, to come and have a look at the girl. When they returned to the house, Jane was on her knees in front of the fire. She looked extremely ill and still unable to speak sensibly, she kept waving her hand at the fire. The neighbours did not understand what Jane was trying to tell them. They could see nothing wrong with the fire as it was burning brightly. Margaret told Simpson he must go for medical help immediately. The two women stayed with Jane and her two-year-old child until Simpson returned. Dr Clarke was not at home so a message had been left with his housekeeper for him to attend as soon as possible. The following day, Simpson went to Jane Thompson to ask for her help in changing his daughter's bed. When Jane Thompson entered the room, Jane Simpson was dressed in one of her father's shirts. The bed she had been lying in was in an awful state. Jane's gown and petticoat were on the kitchen table still wet, having been washed by someone and there were more clothes soaking in the poss tub.

On Thursday morning, Simpson again went to the neighbours for help. Ann Heavisides, Margaret Foulkes and Ann Wilson went into the house. Jane was unconscious, her bedding and clothing were saturated with blood and smelt terrible. The three women changed the linen and stayed in the house. That afternoon Dr Clarke at last arrived. The message he had received from his housekeeper had been to attend Simpson's daughter. The doctor was at the time attending another woman called Simpson, so he had assumed the message was from her. It was only when the doctor received a further message, he realised there had been a mix up.

Shortly after the doctor's arrival, Jane died without regaining consciousness. Dr Clarke told the three neighbours that were in the house that Jane had recently given birth, but where was the child? The women began looking round the house. It did not take them long to find what they were looking for. In the pantry, suspended from a nail was a horse's feeding bag and inside was the badly mutilated body of a baby. The child had been about a month or so premature and had breathed when born. It could not be determined whether it had breathed sufficiently to maintain a separate existence. The body was missing both legs and one arm and parts of the trunk were charred, so badly in fact, that it could not be determined whether the child was male or female. The doctor suspected the child had been dead for about ten or twelve days. Jane Simpson had died from inflammation of the bowel and womb caused by lack of care at her confinement. Because of the poison in her system Jane had developed a fever, which was the cause of her incoherence. It was then realised that when Jane had been waving at the fire she had been trying to tell her neighbours that her baby had been on the fire. The child's missing limbs were never found.

Robert Simpson was arrested and taken into custody at Coxhoe. He was charged with being an accessory to the deaths of his daughter and her baby. Simpson adamantly denied knowing that Jane was pregnant and having anything to do with her or her child's death. Strangely though, he did admit to having slept with her on several occasions. The village women stated at the inquest that Jane had been unhappy and in a very depressed state for months, in fact since the break up of her relationship with Hugh Devon.

The jury found Simpson not guilty because there was not the medical evidence to show that he had contributed to the deaths. Sadly for Jane and her child, Simpson's morals were not on trial or he would surely have been found guilty.

Chapter 12

A Drunken Quarrel
1860

Thomas Smith had worked as a pitman at Whitehaven, Four Stones near Hexham and several mines in the Burnopfield and Pontop districts. He started his working life as a sweep and could also turn his hand to other employment such as husbandry or seamanship. Thomas was a short but powerfully-built man, his face almost blue in colour from a gunpowder explosion a few years previously. He was also well known as being an ardent poacher and having a very good knowledge of the fields and woods. John Baty, a burly, rather stout man, lived in Cuthbert Street, Blaydon. He was known as a good worker, quiet and respectable. Both men were working near to Winlaton but until the night of 5 November they were strangers to one another.

Baty had attended a shooting match at Blaydon Burn and afterwards had gone to *Benwell's* public house in Winlaton. It was here, amongst other company that the two men met. The whole company then moved to *Parker's* where they drank until about twelve-thirty in the morning. Baty, Smith and another man, Armstrong, left the public house together.

At about three that morning, two lads were heading to work down Blaydon Bank when they saw a short distance away, what they thought, was a man asleep. They carried on to work and came upon George Nixon, a manufacturer from Winlaton and told him about the man. Nixon thought he had better go and have a look. On approaching the recumbent figure, Nixon was horrified to see that blood had gushed from a wound on the left temple and the man was dead. Constable James Kelly was notified and a cart was procured to transport the body to the *Commercial Hotel*. The man was identified as John Baty.

Upon a search of the area in which Baty's body had been lying, blood was found on the boundary wall that skirted the footpath. It appeared that it was there the deathblow had been inflicted. Baty must have then staggered a few yards and fallen to the ground. When he was found he was wearing only his shirt, drawers, stockings and neckerchief. The waistcoat, coat, trousers and shoes were missing. In a field nearby the coat and waistcoat were found. There was also a pair of trousers and a pair of shoes that did not belong to the dead man.

On making enquiries, several witnesses came forward. All agreed that the last person to be seen with Baty was Thomas Smith. It was thought that Smith, having already worked at sea, might try to get aboard a ship and leave the country. The following week, however, Smith was apprehended at Whitby. He was wearing the trousers and shoes that had belonged to the dead man. It was soon ascertained that the trousers and shoes found in the field belonged to Smith. The witnesses were called in to identify Smith as the last man to be seen with Baty. Thomas Smith was charged with murder and sent to trial at the Durham Assizes before Justice Keating.

Smith eventually admitted to a drunken argument and said

Blaydon town centre in the early twentieth century. Author's collection

Durham Assizes. The author

that he and John had removed their clothes to fight. Smith's defence argued, that in drink a blow could be delivered with more force than was intended. It was quite logical that they might have removed some of their clothing to fight and it was feasible that in the dark and due to his drunken state, Smith could have picked up the wrong clothes. Baty had not been robbed, as witnesses testified he had no money on his person when he left the public house so what else could it be but a drunken quarrel that went horribly wrong. The blow inflicted on Baty was obviously not pre-meditated so the charge against Smith, if found guilty at all, should be manslaughter not murder. Justice Keating disagreed. He stated that Smith had run away, he had then denied any involvement in the crime; it was only at the eleventh hour he had admitted to striking the blow. An implement, such as a bludgeon had been used, not a fist, to kill Baty, so, therefore, it could not be manslaughter. The jury must either acquit Smith or find him guilty of murder. After a few hours deliberation the jury returned a verdict of guilty. The executioner Thomas Askern hanged Smith on 27 December. Milner Lockey was also hanged that day. (Chapter 10)

Chapter 13

Love Thy Neighbour
1862

lderly people living on their own, especially if a little eccentric, often give rise to rumours of hoarding wealth. Ann Halliday, a lady of eighty-three years, living by herself, was a prime target for such gossip. Her cottage was at a place called Hobbletrot on the Witton Gilbert road. It was about three miles from Chester-le-Street, between Sacriston and Plawsworth.

Ann was married to William Halliday who had formerly been a butcher and publican at the sign of the *Shoulder of Mutton* in Chester-le-Street. The couple had separated some years previously due to Ann's intemperance. With her advancing years, however, she had overcome her drinking habits and led a quiet life. Her husband had procured the cottage at the time of their separation and had provided liberally for Ann ever since.

One Saturday evening in August, Ann had attended a tea party nearby. She spent an enjoyable evening chatting with her neighbours and left for home before it became dark.

Blacksmith's shop, Witton Gilbert. Durham Federation of Women's Institutes and Countryside Books.

About three o'clock on Sunday morning, Ann's husband, William was woken by a knock on his door. He looked out of his window and saw Mary Cox, the wife of an Irishman, John Cox, standing at his door. William shouted down to her 'What do you want?' Mary replied 'That old woman up the road is very bad.' William asked 'What old woman?' She repeated, 'That old woman up the road.' William, although he did not know what the problem was, had a feeling that all was not right and woke his housekeeper and told her to go with Mary and find out what had happened. The housekeeper aroused a neighbour, Mrs Gorby, and the two women followed Mary. She led them to Ann's cottage. On their arrival they found the front door open and John Cox standing outside. When they entered the cottage they were horrified to find Ann lying on the floor in her nightclothes with several ghastly head wounds. She was alive, but only just, and was slipping in and out of consciousness. William's housekeeper and Mrs Gorby tried to get Ann to speak. She mumbled 'oh these Irish' and made some half-hearted gestures. Mrs Gorby had noticed that around the shoulders of Mary Cox was Ann's shawl. The police were sent for and PC Christon attended. He took John Cox over to Ann, who had by now been lifted onto her bed, and asked her if this was the man who had attacked her. Ann's lips moved in what could have been construed as a 'yes'. She died fifteen minutes later at half past six on Sunday morning, just after the surgeon, Mr McCabe, arrived from Witton Gilbert. Dr Hudson of Chester-le-Street attended shortly afterwards. On examination of the body by the two medical men, the injuries were found to be horrific. Fingernail marks were on Ann's neck, as if strangulation had been attempted. The left arm was broken above the elbow; the mark of a heavy blow was on the jugular vein and a severe wound on the left temple. The rest of the elderly woman's body was covered in bruises and marks of extreme violence. Later, on a more detailed examination, it was found also that four of Ann's ribs had been broken, as if she had been jumped upon.

There were two cottages together on a hill overlooking Nettlesworth. One was lived in by Ann and next door lived twenty-five year old John Cox, his wife and young child. Cox worked at Nettlesworth Colliery, he and his family had been

Front Street in Chester-le-Street. Author's collection

living in the cottage for about a month, moving there from Felton. Ann's cottage had a loft above that was hardly used. It had a window that had once had four tiny panes of glass but now had little boards in place of glass. Ann lived and slept in the one room on the ground floor. One odd fact was, that although Ann had died in extremely violent circumstances, the room of the cottage showed no signs of a struggle. Nothing was out of place and there was very little blood on the floor even though her wounds must have bled profusely. A large bloodstain was found on one of the curtains. The conclusion was that Ann had grabbed hold of the curtain during the struggle and the mark was from her bloodstained hand. Another odd fact was that the door key could not be found anywhere. Upon the police searching the tiny cottage, they found the murder weapon. It was a coal rake, the point of which had been driven into Ann's temple. Her chemise was found under the bed, soaking wet, as if it had been washed. The bed was made although her candlestick was at the bedside as if she had retired. A small mahogany chest of drawers showed some signs of having been ransacked. At the end of the bed was a chest in which Ann had kept her linen but it was found to be completely empty. The conclusion was that the linen had been used to clean up the blood and the room had been tidied after the attack. The window in the loft was inspected but no signs of tampering with it were found. Also the squares that now contained pieces of wood were too small for anyone to get through. On the windowsill downstairs was a small pile of books and on the flyleaf of one was written 'Ann Halliday born November 11th 1779 Broadmires near Durham'.

The police arrested Cox and his wife and they were conveyed to Durham gaol. Their young child was taken to the workhouse until matters could be settled. Later the child was given into the care of Mary Cox's brother.

Cox's shirt and trousers were stained with blood. When questioned, he stated that about three o'clock in the morning he had heard the old woman groaning and on going to her door had found it locked. He broke the door open with a poker (the marks on the door verified this) and found Ann on the floor. He had tried to help her and that was how the blood came to be on his clothes. Cox then said he went to his house next door to tell his wife to fetch William Halliday. He then bolted the door from the inside and did not open it again until his wife returned with the two women. Cox stated that someone must have broken in through the window in the loft, robbed and murdered the elderly woman. He could not explain how, although he said the door was locked from the inside, there was no door key found in the cottage.

Mary Cox told her interrogators that Ann's injuries had been caused by her falling out of bed in a fit.

When the Cox's house was searched, there was a large fire burning brightly in the grate. It appeared it had been burning all night and the shovel was upon the fire acting as a draft to fan the flames. What looked like a piece of cloth could be seen on the top.

Cox and his wife appeared at the Durham Winter Assizes in December before Mr Justice Keating. The courtroom was packed with Cox's fellow countrymen. For nearly three hours the defence, Mr Maule, argued that the actions of Cox and his wife were of totally innocent neighbours. Cox's explanation of how the blood came to be on his clothes was feasible. There was no proof that the fire in the Cox's cottage had been burning all night or that there had been anything belonging to Ann upon it. The police had put the fire out and dragged the ashes onto the floor to rake through them. They had found nothing at all. Ann had been heard to say 'oh these Irish' and although Cox and his wife were indeed Irish, there were hundreds of other Irish living and working in the area. PC Christon's evidence that Ann had identified Cox as the man who attacked her should not be admissible as the woman was dying and incoherent at the time. Because of the violence of the attack it had obviously been carried out by a person of some strength, which pointed to the assailant being male. So perhaps in Ann's dying moments, any man who had been put in front of her would have been recognised by her as the perpetrator. Lastly, the defence pointed out that it was not the action of a guilty party to send for help and remain on the scene after a crime had been committed.

Summing up to the jury, Justice Keating pointed out that it was possible that Ann's identification of John Cox was wrong as by that time she would have been wavering in her reason. On the other hand, the statement of a dying person was usually the truth. John had said the door to the cottage was locked but the key was not found. He also said he had bolted the door and had not opened it until his wife and the other two women arrived, yet Mary Cox was wearing Ann's shawl when she went to William Halliday's house for help. Mrs Cox had stated that Ann had fallen from her bed. Was this deliberately meant to mislead? Justice Keating stated that the evidence pointed to John Cox going to Ann Halliday's door on some pretext and being invited in. After he committed the deed, he and his wife tidied the room and mopped up the blood with Ann's linen. They then took the blood soaked linen into their cottage to be burnt. Leaving Ann bleeding to death on the floor, Mary, without thinking, had put Ann's shawl around her shoulders to protect her from the night chill as she supposedly went for help. John, meanwhile, locked the door from the outside then threw the key away before breaking the door open again.

No motive could be found, but speculation pointed to the perpetrators thinking there might be money hidden in the little cottage.

The jury returned after more than two hours with the verdict of guilty of murder on John Cox and guilty of being an accomplice to murder on Mary Cox. At this Mary Cox called out in a plaintive tone. 'My Lord, I throw myself in your hands. I had nothing at all to do with it. I had nothing to do with it.'

Justice Keating pronounced sentence of death upon them both and at that chaos ensued in the courtroom. Mary Cox began wailing and then appearing to become hysterical she rushed towards her husband. Everyone in the courtroom stood to see what was going on and the authorities though that an attempt might be made to free the prisoners. The doors were quickly bolted and Cox was dragged, resisting violently and swearing blasphemously, down the steps from the dock. The officers of the court were occupied in keeping the more demonstrative Irishmen under control. When order was restored it transpired that Mary Cox had told a female warder that she was pregnant. Justice Keating ordered that twelve matrons take her to a room to ascertain whether this was true. Mary was found to be pregnant so Justice Keating ordered a stay of execution until after her confinement. Her sentence was later changed to life in penal servitude.

Cox protested his innocence to the end. This came on the morning of 23 December 1862. The day dawned with clear blue skies, more like a day in spring than winter. At nine o'clock, Thomas Askern, the executioner performed his duty to the sound of Mary Cox wailing from another part of the prison. Cox's body was left hanging for an hour before being taken down and interred within the prison walls.

Mary Cox's brother, who had taken in their child, also had four of his own children. He was paid the sum of 1s 6d (7.5p) for the upkeep of the child. Owing to the scandal surrounding his relatives, he had moved from Chester-le-Street. Because it was not worth his while to travel back to collect this small sum every week he wanted rid of the child. Eventually the child was placed in a workhouse.

Condemned man's cell. Author's collection

Chapter 14

Gunpowder and Rum
1866

At the Durham Winter Assizes in December the case against Henry Brownless, a pitman, caused considerable interest. The accused appeared in the dock dressed in a black suit with a scarlet muffler around his neck. The muffler was to conceal the deep marks caused by an attempt he had made to cut his own throat.

Henry, his son, also called Henry and Mary Ann, his son's wife lived in a tiny house in Houghton-le-Spring. The house consisted of a front room, kitchen, pantry and a yard to the ground floor. A ladder leading from the front room reached a bedroom on the second floor where Brownless slept. His son and his daughter in law slept in the front room.

Brownless and his daughter-in-law, Mary Ann, did not get on and on 10 October things came to a head. Brownless was drunk and had called Mary Ann a bad name and then struck her. His son threatened to take him before the magistrates but had second thoughts and instead he and Mary Ann left the house to stay elsewhere.

The following day Brownless apologised to the couple and pleaded with them to return to the house saying that his actions were due to drink and it would not happen again. The couple relented and returned to the little house.

All went well with the family until Thursday 18 October. At about three o'clock in the afternoon, Brownless, who was in his room upstairs, shouted to Mary Ann to dry his stockings and bring them to him. When she delivered the stockings, he then told her to fetch him a pot of rum. Mary Ann left to do his bidding. When she returned Brownless was sitting downstairs reading a newspaper. She gave him the rum and went about her chores. Putting some potatoes on the fire to boil, Mary Ann stirred the fire with the poker and then put it on the fender in its usual place. Brownless then asked her to get him another pot of rum. Once again Mary Ann did as she was bid going out through the back door and leaving the front door open. When she returned with the rum there were two gill glasses and a wine glass on the table. Brownless then told Mary Ann to shout for Mrs Reid from next door to come and have a drink with him. Mary Ann shouted to Mrs Reid and then went to see to the potatoes, noticing at the same time that the poker was now in the fire and three quarters of the thick end of it was red hot.

In the course of their work pitmen often used gunpowder and Brownless was in possession of 20 lbs (about 7 kilograms). This was stored in a barrel that stood about six feet (2 metres) from the fireplace.

Mrs Reid came in through the back door. Brownless invited her to sit down and have a sup with him, as 'she was a hearty woman'. Mary Ann was standing on one side of the fire and Brownless was on the other. Suddenly he seized Mary Ann's dress with his left hand and snatched the poker from the fire with his right and applied it to the barrel of gunpowder. What followed was utter chaos. Brownless kept hold of Mary Ann's dress until it gave way at the back. She then, with her dress in flames, tried to leave by the front door but he had bolted it and it took her a minute or two before she managed to open it. The roof of the building had been blown off and the rear pantry was in ruins. Barely conscious, Mrs Reid managed to stagger out through what had once been the pantry window. As she got outside, she realised her three-year-old daughter, Anne Maria, was in her arms. The little girl had followed her mother into the house and got caught up in the explosion. Anne Maria's clothes were in flames and there was blood running down her face.

Neighbours had heard the explosion and came running to the house. William Holmes, also a pitman, arrived at the scene first. He tore the burning clothes from the two women and the child's bodies and then entered what was left of the house. Brownless was on his knees on the floor bleeding from the neck. William tried to lift him but Brownless would not co-operate. Being overcome by the smoke, William then left the building. Other neighbours eventually managed to get Brownless out of the house. He then asked how his two enemies were getting on, presumably meaning his daughter-in-law and Mrs Reid. He then said he wanted to die with them.

Meanwhile the victims had received medical attention. Both Mary Ann and Mrs Reid were severely burnt. Mary Ann lost her sight for nine days. Little Anne Maria died minutes after the explosion.

Brownless' plan had 'backfired' so to speak. Not only had he murdered a child instead of the victims he intended, he had also failed to take his own life. He was charged with the murder of Anne Maria Reid.

On 8 December at Durham Winter Assizes before Justice Lush, Brownless was found guilty of murder and sentenced to death. A question arose from the jury about Brownless' sanity and if he was fit to plead. They queried how such a small amount of rum caused him to become so drunk that he would perpetrate this terrible crime? No date was set for the execution and Justice Lush ordered Brownless to be kept in strict custody until he thought about the issue. The peculiar circumstances of the crime were said to weigh heavily on Justice Lush's mind. He contacted Whitehall and on 18 December received a reply. The Queen ordered a respite of the sentence and that Brownless be instead detained at Her Majesty's Pleasure.

Chapter 15

No Evidence
1866

Jane Craggs, who was fifty, had been living apart from her husband for some time. She had been acting as housekeeper to seventy-five year old James Cooper, a pitman. They lived in a small cottage in Easington Lane, about six miles from Durham. The cottage consisted of a room on the ground floor, occupied by Cooper, and another room above which was reached by a ladder where Craggs slept. At the back of the cottage was a garden in which Cooper grew a few vegetables. Cooper's room had a large, curtained four-poster bed.

At the beginning of May it was known that employer and employee had fallen out over some matter. Craggs was heard to say that she would get rid of Cooper by giving him something to send him off. On 13 May Cooper bought some cabbage plants and was seen planting them in his garden. At the time he was wearing a pair of light brown corduroy trousers. The following day he was missed and a little girl knocked at his door. Receiving no answer she peeped through the keyhole and saw a fire burning in the grate and the curtains drawn around the bed.

On 15 May Craggs was seen in the street apparently in tears. When a neighbour, Mrs Ridley, asked what was wrong Craggs replied that she had a sore eye. Mrs Ridley then asked if Cooper was well. Craggs replied that he was fine and that he had gone to Coxhoe on the previous day. That afternoon a servant girl from the *Three Tops* public house went to Cooper's to fetch a barrow for her master. As she passed through the garden she noticed a very disagreeable smell coming from the house. On entering the cottage she saw the curtains were drawn around the bed and Craggs was beside the fire trying to stoke it with the poker. She was incapable of doing so because she was very drunk. The servant stirred the fire for Craggs and then lifted the

Durham in 2002. The author

candle and looked towards the bed. She commented on it being 'a queer old bed' to which Craggs replied that 'it is a damp old bed too'.

Suspicions were aroused in the village when Cooper had not appeared at the colliery to work for almost a week. A fellow pitman, James Kirkley, asked Craggs about Cooper's absence. When she said he had gone to Coxhoe, Kirkley asked if Cooper had any money. Craggs said he had 6s (30p) of his own and she had lent him 7s (35p). Kirkley was not satisfied with this and asked to look at the bed. Craggs refused to allow him to do so. Kirkley went to get two of his friends and a police officer. He was away about an hour and it was later thought that this would have given Craggs time to destroy any incriminating evidence.

When the four men arrived back at the cottage Craggs still insisted that Cooper had gone to Coxhoe. The police officer pushed past her and pulled open the bed curtains. Decomposing on the bed was Cooper's body. There was blood spattered on the pillow and the bedcovers that looked as though it had come from Cooper's nose. His jugular vein and the side of his neck was bruised and swollen. His tongue was protruding from his mouth and his eyes were open and dilated. It looked very much as though he had been strangled. Craggs insisted that she had not known that the body was there, she thought Cooper had not returned from Coxhoe. Cooper's corduroy trousers were missing but seven buttons were found in the fire grate. There was, however, no proof that the buttons came from the trousers. Had Craggs burnt the trousers for some reason known only to her?

Craggs was arrested and an inquest held. Two medical men were brought in to examine the body. Their opinions differed. One thought death was caused by the man being seized by the throat and strangled. The other thought because of Cooper's age, he had died from natural causes. The judge addressed the jury saying it was a rule that a murder must be proven to have been committed before any accusations against a person could be made. Because of the conflicting medical opinions the jury decided there was not enough evidence to show that a murder had taken place and Jane Craggs walked free.

Chapter 16

A Mysterious Death
1869

Mary Brown was twenty-two and worked as a servant for Mr Kirkup of Hill Side Farm at Pittington. She was about to leave her situation to be married to George Perrot who also worked for Mr Kirkup.

On 22 April a neighbour, Mrs Weighall, entered the scullery of the farmhouse to find Mary giddy and unbalanced. Mrs Weighall assisted the girl to bed and sent for Dr A J E Parker from Easington Lane. By the time the doctor arrived Mary was very lethargic. Dr Parker applied some vinegar to Mary's eyes whereupon she became a little livelier. Her skin was cold and clammy and she kept drifting off to sleep. The doctor suspected that she might have taken opium. He tried to give her coffee but she could not swallow. Later that evening Mary died. Dr Parker thought all the symptoms pointed to her death being caused by some sort of poison.

Dr Parker and a colleague, Mr Buston, had carried out a post-mortem and although they both believed the cause of death to be poison they could find no traces in the body. They mixed some of the contents of the stomach with milk and cream and fed it to two cats. The cats did not take much of the mixture, as they seemed to find it distasteful. Neither cat suffered any ill effects from the little they did eat. Some of the stomach contents were sent to a chemist for analysis. The doctors did find that Mary was just over three months pregnant with twin boys.

An inquest was held at the *Bonnie Pit Laddie* public house in Pittington. The first witness to be called was Phillis Brown, Mary's aunt. Phillis thought that Mr Kirkup had put poison in Mary's dinner. She said that Mary had told her that Mr Kirkup had offered her things to let him take liberties with her. When Mary told her this, Phillis wanted her to leave the farm straight away but Mary said she was leaving soon anyway so she may as well get her wages for the short time she had left to work.

George Perrot was next to be called as a witness. He said that he, another worker and Mary had all eaten the same for their dinner and the two men had suffered no ill effects. Mary had told George about her master making suggestions to her and he had wanted to have words with Mr Kirkup. Mary had asked him not to as it would only cause trouble and she would be leaving soon anyway. George had known Mary was pregnant and he said he was the father. He also said that Mary had received three 'very bad' letters lately and that her aunt, Phillis had two of them, the other had been destroyed. Phillis produced one of the letters and the coroner read the contents. It seemed to be from a jealous woman. The coroner then told the jury that the letter was bad and could not be read out but felt it had nothing to do with the case at hand anyway. Mr Kirkup was then called. He denied the accusations and said that they were staining his character. The inquest was adjourned for a fortnight.

When the inquest was resumed it was pointed out that Mr Kirkup had been informed of Mary's illness but instead of notifying Phillis of her niece's plight, he went to Sunderland and did not return until after Mary's death. When he was told of his servant's death he said 'she must have poisoned herself'. The coroner was also told that Mr and Mrs Kirkup's daughter had died a little while previously. Before her death she had been taking morphia to ease her pain. No bottles of morphia were found in the house. It was then suggested that perhaps Mary had been told to take morphia to Miss Kirkup at some time and had kept some back but if this were so, then where was the bottle? The only thing that was found was a small amount of a mixture of laudanum and chloroform that Mary had once used to ease a toothache.

The chemist who analysed the stomach contents could find no trace of poison. He said this could be because there was a lapse of two days after death before the samples were taken and any traces may have disappeared by then.

The verdict of the jury was, as poison was not found in the system there was no evidence to show the true cause of death. There was also not enough evidence to show whether Mary had taken her own life or to implicate Mr Kirkup in her death. The inquest was then terminated.

Chapter 17

The Long Arm of the Law

Pittington, 1868

Constable David Paton and Constable John Cruikshanks were both members of the Durham Police Constabulary. Both men originated from Scotland and were married with families. Paton, who had been stationed at Sherburn, had been found guilty of some irregularities concerning his conduct at work. Cruikshanks, who had been stationed at Pittington close to Sherburn, had gone to his superior officer and reported his colleague. Due to Cruikshanks' evidence Paton was ordered to appear before Lieutenant-Colonel White. The ensuing investigation resulted in Paton being discharged from the constabulary.

The same afternoon that Paton was expelled from his position

An engine near Pittington in 1844 by T H Hair. Durham Mining Museum

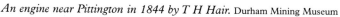

in the police force, Cruikshanks and a man named McKay left Durham to head home. A short while after five Paton joined the two men. When they reached Sherburn Bridge Cruikshanks wanted to walk down the Sunderland and Durham Railway line, as it was the shortest route to his house, which was situated just outside the village. Paton, however, said that he had some information from the Durham Constabulary office in his house that he wished to hand over to Cruikshanks. Accordingly the three men continued towards Paton's house within the village. Cruikshanks waited at a distance of about thirty yards (eleven metres) away while Paton went to his house with McKay following him. Mc Kay wanted to collect his *Police Gazetteer*. McKay entered the house and sat down. Cruikshanks saw Paton come out of the house by the back kitchen door, his right arm behind his back. Paton's wife shouted 'He has something!' McKay jumped up and looked out of the window to see Cruikshanks running down the road towards Thompson's public house with Paton chasing after him. Going to the door, McKay saw Paton shoot Cruikshanks twice as he tried to enter the public house. McKay ran towards them but as he did so, Paton put the pistol to his right ear and pulled the trigger. McKay caught him as he fell. Mr Shaw, a surgeon was called immediately but when he arrived Cruikshanks was already dead and Paton died a few minutes later.

At the inquest the jury returned a verdict of wilful murder against Paton and a verdict of suicide on Paton's own death. Whether sane or insane there was not enough evidence to show.

Tow Law: 1876

Joseph Christison was a member of the Durham County Constabulary and was stationed a short distance from Tow Law. There were races taking place at Tow Law on the 29 May so Christison and another police officer, Watson, were granted leave of absence to attend. They spent most of the day at the races and were already very drunk when they left. In fact Christison said he could not remember anything after about six o'clock.

High Street, Tow Law. Author's collection

At midnight a loud knocking at his door woke the landlord of the *Traveller's Rest*. On looking out of the window, the landlord, Howe, saw Christison standing outside with two sticks in his hand. He was shouting to be let in. Howe refused and Christison went to the back of the building and began breaking the windows. Howe ran downstairs, by this time Christison was walking away from the public house. Howe followed him and then saw, coming towards him, John Hamill. Hamill was bleeding profusely from wounds to his head and could barely walk upright. He pointed in the direction Christison had gone and said 'he has done this.' Howe took Hamill to the public house and called for some help from the neighbours. While they were trying to staunch Hamill's wounds, Christison entered. In his hand were two large sticks. One of the sticks had a large round knob at the end and this appeared to be covered with blood. Hamill pointed to Christison and said 'he has done this.' Christison then calmly took a white handkerchief from his pocket and wiped the blood from the end of the stick. Howe and his neighbours locked the door and endeavored to secure Christison. Suddenly there was the sound of breaking glass and a hammering on the door. The door was smashed open and in came Watson. A scuffle ensued and the villagers managed to handcuff the two policemen and take them to Consett. The stick with the blood on the end disappeared at some time during the chaos and was never seen again.

Hamill died of his injuries on 31 May. A post-mortem showed that his skull was fractured in two places. One of the blows was most certainly caused by the rounded object on the end of a stick that had been described by witnesses. The other could have been from a fall on a stone. On enquiries being made it was proven that Hamill had walked quite a long way after receiving his injuries. He had stopped at a few public houses and partook of small quantities of spirits in each one. He had been heading towards Tow Law to complain to the magistrate of what had happened to him.

A large number of people, including tradesmen and the police superintendent, came forward as character witnesses for Christison as to his sobriety and attention to duty. The defence stated that the evidence for the prosecution was purely circumstantial and that Hamill travelling so far the day he was supposed to have been attacked accelerated death.

After an hour's deliberation the jury returned a verdict of guilty of manslaughter. Justice Lush sentenced Christison to twenty years penal servitude. Before leaving Durham, Justice Lush reconsidered the sentence and changed it to fifteen years.

Butterknowle: 1884

Sergeant William Smith, who was stationed at Butterknowle Colliery, had been enjoying a drink with Robert Lamb, a butcher, at the *Royal Oak Inn* in Butterknowle on the evening of 24 February. They bade each other goodnight at about ten o'clock in the evening. Mr G Gorrick, who was an assistant to Dr Middleton was in the area when a young man came up to him and said there was a policeman dead upon the road. Mr Gorrick went to the engine house to fetch Dr Middleton and they found Smith lying in the gutter, barely alive, with his head bashed in. The doctor and his assistant looked for the young man that had discovered the policeman but he was nowhere to be seen. They did, however, see three men disappearing into the distance. Smith was removed to his house where he died shortly afterwards. Violent blows to the head, causing multiple, severe fractures to the skull had caused his death. A shirt button, large stones and a brick covered in blood were found near to the scene.

The police brought a few men in for questioning. Dr

Butterknowle in the early twentieth century.. Author's collection

Middleton and his assistant went to both Staindrop and Barnard Castle police stations to see if they could identify any of the three men seen that night. They picked out three men who were similar in height and build to the three seen. The police arrested Joseph Lowson, twenty-five, William Siddle, twenty-five and Joseph Hodgson, twenty-eight, on the witness identifications.

At the ensuing inquest held at the *Royal Oak Inn*, other witnesses came forward. William Taylor, a woodsman from Staindrop, had accompanied Sergeant Daley to where Smith

Staindrop Church Author's collection

had been found. He saw the sergeant find the button. They, along with another police officer, Constable Lewis, then picked up Joseph Lowson and took him to the police station. There was a button missing from Lowson's shirt. On the way to the police station Lowson had said to Taylor 'I hope we have not murdered him Bill'. Constable Lewis heard Lowson speak and asked 'what's that my man'? Lowson then kept quiet. Taylor also said he noticed a spot of blood on Lowson's cheek. Taylor was asked why he had not mentioned Lowson's remark or the blood on Lowson's cheek in his initial statement. He replied that he did not think it was of any importance.

William Alkman, who lived at Abbot's Houses, was walking near the engine house on the night of the murder. He had seen three men at about ten o'clock and another three men just afterwards. The last three seemed to be in earnest conversation and very drunk. As they passed Alkman, one of them brushed against him. A little further on Alkman passed a policeman who was heading in the same direction as the men. That same night Alkman heard about the murder. He later identified one of the men held at the police station as being the same stature as one of the three that had brushed against him that night.

John Simpson, landlord of the *Diamond Inn* at Butterknowle, said there had been a 'pigeon shooting' at his place on the day of the murder. The three accused men were at the inn that night. Hodgson and Siddle were in the parlour and Lowson was in one of the other rooms. Siddle did not stay long. There were about seventy people there altogether.

Ralph Blackett, innkeeper of Evenwood and Francis Morrell, labourer said they thought they had seen Siddle near the scene of the murder at closing time, but it was a very dark night and there had been a lot of people about. George Hutchinson, cartman, said that in the previous July he had been in the *Diamond Inn* when he had been witness to an altercation. Siddle, who was the worse for drink was threatening to thrash Sergeant Smith.

The county analyst examined the shirts belonging to the accused men. On one was found a stain that he thought may have been blood but whether human or animal he could not be

Brown Jug Inn *at Evenwood Gate near Evenwood.* The author

sure. The shirt that was stained belonged to Lowson.

The defence pointed out that Dr Middleton and his assistant Mr Gorrick had been drinking all evening and, therefore, their eyesight would not have been perfect. Also the button that was found was a common one and could have come from any shirt. The evidence was all circumstantial.

The three men were committed for trial to the Durham Assizes on 3 May before Justice Hawkins. The evidence was

Northgate in Darlington. Author's collection

repeated and the jury retired to consider their verdict. Hodgson was found not guilty, Lowson and Siddle guilty. Both men protested their innocence denying any part in Smith's death. Justice Hawkins said that he thought the jury had come to a right and conscientious verdict and pronounced sentence of death on both men.

During the following weeks the mining community of the county held meetings with the object of obtaining a reprieve. Siddle wrote a letter to the Home Secretary. The effect of this was that the prisoners received a week's respite while a treasury official made a searching enquiry at Darlington and Barnard Castle into the accuracy of the contents of the letter. The result from the Home Secretary was a reprieve during Her Majesty's Pleasure for Siddle but not for Lowson. A week before Lowson's death penalty was to be carried out he issued a statement confessing his guilt but alleging that Siddle had nothing to do with the crime, and indeed, had tried to stop the attack. Ralph Blackett received a communication from Lowson saying that Hodgson had been the one to instigate the murderous attack on Sergeant Smith.

As James Berry, the executioner, was about to put the white cap over Lowson's head on the morning of 27 May 1884, Lowson said,

> *I wish to say that Hodgson struck the first blow and then I helped him. I hope that the Crown and county will look after Siddle and send him safe home again.*

Lowson had six brothers, three sisters, a wife and children. He had written a letter to one of his brothers, Richard, on 24 May. Richard received the letter after Lowson's death. In the letter there was an apology to his family for what he had done and it was repeated that it was Hodgson and not Siddle who had been his partner in crime. Lowson also wrote that there was not much time left to him. If only Hodgson would come forward and tell the truth it might help him but he thought that by now Hodgson would be long gone from the area.

James Berry,
executioner from 1884-92.
Author's collection

Chapter 18

A Beating at Spennymoor
1872

Jane and Joseph Waine lived with their son and a lodger at Duncombe Street in Spennymoor. Next door lived John Hayes, his wife and son and two lodgers, George Beasley and Terence Rice; the two houses were separated only by a narrow passage. Jane later gave her version of the events that took place at her house late on the night of Saturday, 16 November.

Hugh Slane came in by the back door to ask Jane for some matches, which she sold for a little extra income. Jane gave him the matches and as she did so Slane noticed the lodger, whose name was Wilson, sitting by the fire. Slane asked Wilson if he was the man who had been at *Carrick's Beerhouse* that night. Wilson replied that he had no money for drink and as he was a stranger in the town, did not know where *Carrick's Beerhouse* was. Slane became angry and called him a liar. Joseph Waine told Slane that Wilson was telling the truth; he had never left the house all night. Slane became even angrier and called him a liar too, then went into the back lane shouting for Waine to come out. Waine ignored him and filled his pipe then stood at the front door smoking it. Suddenly Slane appeared and throwing the box of matches into Waine's face, grabbed him by the jacket collar and dragged him into the side passage. Jane followed them trying to get Slane to let her husband go. Hayes, Beasley and Rice all came from next door into the passage when they heard the commotion. Slane held his victim down while the others commenced to kick him. Jane managed to pull Rice away from her husband but Hayes got hold of her and pulled her cap and shawl off and pushed her out of the passage. Hayes then took a running kick at Waine who was still lying on the floor. The four men then went into Hayes' house. Wilson helped Waine into the house and put him on the bed that was in the front kitchen. Jane

Vulcan Hotel *at Spennymoor.* Author's collection

went to get the police and as she left the house the four men came out. Hayes approached with the intention of hitting her and Rice ran forward to kick her but two men that were passing stopped them.

A neighbour, Mary Maughan who lived at 22 George Street, went for a doctor at Waine's request. The doctor prescribed salt water and mustard to make Waine sick but the treatment was to no avail and he died about midnight. Before he died he made no mention to the police as to who had attacked him. The police arrested the four men on Jane's evidence and they were sent to stand trial for murder.

At the Durham Assizes Justice Denham found all four men guilty and condemned them to death. The sentence was to be carried out on 6 January 1873. Efforts were made to obtain a commutation of the sentence on Slane, Hayes and Rice and a remission for Beasley. Slane, Hayes and Rice insisted that Beasley was not involved in the attack. The sentence on Beasley and Rice was commuted to life in penal servitude. On 13 January 1873, William Calcraft carried out the sentence of death on Hugh Slane and John Hayes.

The fight to have Beasley and Rice released carried on and in March of 1877, Mr Joseph Rowntree a member of the Society of Friends, appeared in Bishop Auckland Police Court armed with new evidence. Mary Ann Maher of Back Duncombe Street stated that she was at John Hayes's house on 16 November. Shortly after she arrived George Beasley and John Hayes came into the house from the theatre. They were in a state of intoxication and Mrs Hayes said they could lie down on the bed in the front room. They both fell asleep and did not wake until the police knocked on the door. Mrs Hayes collaborated Mary Ann's story and added that Terence Rice had been bottling ginger beer in her house all night until the police arrived. Her son, Joseph Hayes, also collaborated the stories. At the time of the trial they were not allowed to give evidence because they were too closely related to the accused.

I could find no further records pertaining to this case but it is very probable that the two men remained incarcerated for life.

Chapter 19

Victims of Passion and Abuse

Winlaton, 1865

Coming up to Christmas, the month of December should have brought happy anticipation, not so for one pitman's wife. In the village of Spen, near Winlaton, on 17 December she suffered death at the hands of her abusive and brutal husband.

Matthew Atkinson had been at a shooting match most of the day and had consumed a large amount of alcohol. When he returned home in the late evening his wife, Ellen, had already retired to bed. Atkinson knocked at the door and she arose to let him in. When Ellen opened the door, she was half asleep and Atkinson assumed her appearance to mean she was drunk. He seized the fire irons and beat his wife about the head and body with them. Becoming exhausted with his exertions, Atkinson went outside to recover himself. Regaining his strength he went back into the house and resumed the attack. Using the heavy weapon he continued beating his wife again and again until she was dead and so badly mutilated that she hardly resembled a human being. Neighbours had heard the poor woman's screams but had taken no notice because Atkinson often beat her.

The murderer was taken into custody and tried at the following Durham Assizes before Justice Mellor. Convicted of the brutal murder of his wife, Atkinson was executed by Askern on 16 March 1865. The rope broke after the drop had fallen and twenty minutes were to elapse before another rope was procured and the sentence was carried out. During the wait Atkinson told those around him that he had a premonition that the rope would break. His execution was the last in Durham to be carried out in public.

Brandon Colliery: 1875

Sarah Forster was nineteen when her twenty-two year old lover George Plummer (alias Harding) killed her. Sarah lived with her father and sister at Chester Moor and Plummer lived with his parents at Brandon Colliery. The couple had been courting for almost a year when they became engaged.

On Monday afternoon of the week they were to be married the couple had gone for their dinner to Plummer's house. Plummer suddenly withdrew a revolver from his pocket and fired two shots at Sarah. The unsuspecting girl had her back turned to him at the time. The first shot caught her in the back of the head, probably killing her instantly. When Sarah fell to the floor, Plummer fired again, this time into her mouth. The young man then made good his escape.

The police, on foot and on horseback, set out to search for the culprit, but not finding any trace of him on Monday night, the local people assumed that Plummer had probably taken his own life. It transpired that he had gone at first to some of the colliery villages in the Browney and Darensa Valleys, then to Ushaw Moor and Steatburn before retracing his steps to Brandon Colliery. It was not far from the scene of the murder where he was eventually apprehended. A huge crowd had gathered in the village and as the afternoon went into evening and workmen finished their labour the numbers swelled. A local on the outskirts of the crowd, by the name of Thomas Green, was standing near a privy when he saw the door open and someone peep out and then hurriedly shut the door again. Recognising Plummer he ran to the privy and held the latch of the door closed and shouted for help. The large crowd gathered around the privy and the police had to push their way through to arrest the man. Through the booing and hissing villagers, Plummer was led to the *Brancepeth Castle Hotel*. A conveyance was obtained and he was transported to Durham gaol. Along the length of the road to Stone Bridge the crowd continued to yell at the prisoner.

When Plummer was searched, two brand new, very fancy revolvers were found fully loaded, one of which had been fired recently.

Joseph Forster, Sarah's father, stated that a neighbour of his, a young man named Coates, had shown an interest in Sarah but since she had met Plummer she had eyes for no one else. Forster knew that Plummer had suffered poor health in the past but had seen no sign of depression or fits.

Brancepeth Castle. Author's collection

Plummer's mother, Mrs Harding, had been present at the time of the shooting. She said the couple had not been quarrelling and she could see no reason why her son had done such a thing. Mrs Plummer also said her son had had poor health, restlessness, loss of memory and broken sleep for years. He had given up all his interests except his great love of firearms. Uriah Harding, Plummer's father, said that he knew his son's mind was wrong but did not tell the Forsters because he wanted the marriage to take place.

Dr Boyd examined Plummer and found him to be in poor medical health but not insane. He felt that the prisoner knew exactly what he was doing when he carried out the murder. Plummer was then committed to the Durham Assizes for trial. Plummer's uncle, Francis Ford, gave evidence at the trial. He stated that his nephew had grown very forgetful and did not care about his appearance. Ford also stated that a short while previously Plummer had pulled a loaded revolver out of his pocket, half cocked it, held it to his head and said 'Eh' and then 'I wish I were dead and then I would be out of the road'. Ford said that he had often spoken to his nephew about his illness and about the danger of carrying firearms.

The Winterton section of the Sedgefield Lunatic Asylum. Author's collection

Robert Smith, a doctor and a member of the Royal College of Surgeons who practiced as superintendent of Sedgefield Lunatic Asylum, was next to give evidence. He testified that Plummer had been suffering from melancholia for a number of months prior to the shooting. Dr Smith had been dealing with cases of insanity for twenty-two years and had 700 patients under his charge. It was his opinion that insanity resulted from disease in the digestive organs and Plummer was not a healthy man. Dr Smith stated that a sudden maniacal attack could stem from melancholia and that the person would not be conscious of the nature or the consequences of such an act.

The jury were instructed that they must decide whether Plummer was sane when he shot Sarah Forster and, therefore, guilty of murder. If they decided he was insane then they must find him not guilty. After an hour and twenty minutes of deliberation the jury returned a verdict of not guilty due to insanity. Plummer was then ordered to be detained in a lunatic asylum at Her Majesty's Pleasure. The crowds that were waiting outside had not heard Dr Smith's evidence and were, at first, shocked at the verdict of not guilty. Even once word got round that Plummer had been found insane, it was still felt by the majority that he should have hanged for the taking of such a young girl's life.

Edmondsley: 1876
On Friday 23 June, John Williams, a miner, was in bed when one of his sons brought the wages home from the pit. The family earnings amounted to about £6 a week. Williams stayed in bed until about seven in the evening. He then took a half sovereign from the wages and took himself off to the *Black Dene* public house. His wife, concerned at the amount of money he had taken, followed him. Williams was annoyed at this and after having a few drinks returned home at about nine thirty that evening. He took a gun from the house and after loading it, went in search of his wife. She was hiding in the public house and when the landlord saw the temper Williams was in and the gun, he refused him admittance. After waiting outside for a while, he gave up and returned home. Mrs Williams went for her two brothers, Joseph and John Wales, and told them what had happened. She told them that she was too frightened to return home so they agreed to go and try to calm her husband. On entering the house they tried to persuade Williams to put the gun down. He was, however, beyond reason and stepping back put the gun to his shoulder. Joseph Wales exclaimed 'Williams you are surely not going to fire!' Williams answered 'Stand by or I'll shoot you' and with that the gun discharged. The charge struck John Wales on the right arm and shoulder, and the ramrod, which had not been withdrawn from the barrel, passed through the right lung and struck the spine. He died the following day.

In July, Justice Lush pronounced sentence of death on John Williams for the murder of his brother-in-law. His Lordship pointed out that this was another dreadful illustration of what drink could produce. William Marwood hanged Williams on 6 July 1876.

Evenwood: 1880
Elizabeth Holmes came from a well-respected family. Her parents had kept public houses at South Church and Carmen Hill, both suburbs in Bishop Auckland. Elizabeth lived with her twin sister and her sister's husband, James Mills, a miner. At twenty-five years old she was of short, stout stature and worked for Ralph Vart of Buck Head at Evenwood as a farm servant in the fields.

Elizabeth had been keeping company for some time with

An old farm building on the road to Evenwood. The author

William Brownless. He was a powerful young man of twenty-two, a shoemaker by trade, who worked for Robert Shaw of Butterknowle. Brownless was known in the area as a good-for-nothing. He drank heavily and was violent in drink. Another reason for the local's dislike of the man was that he had broken into Mrs Joplin's drapery store and had spent three months in prison for the crime.

After spending some time with Brownless one evening, Elizabeth returned to her brother-in-law's house and told her family that she would not be seeing the young man again. She had ended the relationship but gave her family no explanation as to why.

The following morning Elizabeth set off for work just before eight, carrying a hoe and a satchel containing her dinner. Her route took her along a footpath leading to Cockfield. About nine thirty, a young man, William Teesdale, who was looking for employment walked the same route. Where the footpath crossed a field he saw two bodies lying in a pool of blood. The woman was dead but the man moved his eyes. Horrified by the spectacle he ran to get help. There were workers in the adjoining field and Teesdale told them of the discovery. The field belonged to Mr Vart, Elizabeth's employer, who immediately sent a cart to

A cobbler or shoemaker working in his shop in the nineteenth century.
Pattison's Pictures, Bowes Museum

convey the dead woman and the man to Evenwood. The woman was Elizabeth Holmes and the man William Brownless. The body of Elizabeth was taken to her family's house and Brownless, barely alive, was taken to the *Drover's Inn* kept by Mr W Vaughan. Two doctors and Superintendent Banks of the county police at Bishop Auckland were sent for. Elizabeth's throat had been cut from ear to ear completely severing the windpipe. There were also two other gashes to her throat that were thought to have been first attempts that did not succeed. William's throat had been cut twice; he had lost a large quantity of blood and was almost comatose. Around the scene of the crime there was trampled grass and blood spread about in all directions showing that there had been a fearful struggle. Elizabeth's bonnet, hoe, shawl and satchel and a man's hat were all found in different places. Strangely, there had been women working in a field nearby but they had not heard or seen anything.

Brownless, although it was touch and go, survived, the doctors said that this was probably due to the efforts of Mr Vart. He had tied a handkerchief around Brownless' throat to stem the flow of blood before taking him on the cart to Evenwood. Once he could speak, Brownless asked if Elizabeth was alive and because he was in such a precarious state of health, was told she was. He then proceeded to relate what had happened. Brownless knew the path Elizabeth took to work and had been hiding behind a hedge waiting for her. As she passed he pulled her down by the legs. Managing to struggle to her feet, Elizabeth ran a few yards into the field. Brownless had caught up with her and drew a razor across her throat, he then changed the razor to the other hand and drew it back across her throat in the opposite

Evenwood in 1916. Author's collection

direction before cutting his own throat. The police and the doctors thought a shoemaker's knife had been used but Brownless insisted it was a razor and that he had not thrown it away. The weapon was not found, either at the scene or on the man's person.

Eventually standing trial for murder, Brownless was condemned to death by Judge Field and hanged on 16 November 1880 by William Marwood. A report of the hanging stated that the large gash on Brownless' throat had not completely healed. Not concerned about this fact, Marwood gave him a nine-foot drop and the rope imbedded itself so deeply into the gash it almost severed the head. Witnesses said 'this presented a shocking appearance after death.'

Silksworth: 1883
Elizabeth Ann Sharp was only eighteen when she married in January of 1883. Her husband was a seagoing fireman, James Burton, who was thirty-three. A few weeks into the marriage, Elizabeth left to go into service for Mr Brewis, a solicitor at Sunderland. She had left because of the ill treatment she received from her new husband and she had also discovered that he still had a wife living elsewhere.

On 8 May Elizabeth and James met, according to Burton to try and patch things up between them. The couple set off walking towards Silksworth when witnesses heard a scream coming from a bridge over which the Ryhope and Silksworth railway passed. Elizabeth was then seen running up the railway embankment with Burton chasing after her. Just after eight that morning, John Stevenson an engine driver, saw an umbrella lying on the railway line. Stopping for a closer look he saw the body of a young woman beside the line. The head had been battered in with a stone. The body was lying face down with five large pieces of limestone placed on the torso and three on the head. The young woman was Elizabeth Burton.

A search was immediately conducted to find her husband. James Burton was apprehended in Sunderland, his clothes were covered in blood and in his pocket were two empty laudanum bottles. The initial inquest was held at the *Half Moon* and he was committed to trial at Durham. Burton was found guilty of

William Marwood, executioner from 1874-83.
Brian Elliott

murder and condemned to die by Justice Hawkins. He left a confession to be read after his death. The confession stated that on that fateful day he had begged his wife to return to him but she had refused. Burton said that Elizabeth had dropped something while they were talking and when he had picked the item up to return it to her she had poked him with an umbrella. Burton had lost his temper and hit Elizabeth then picked up a stone and hit her with it. When he realised she was dead, Burton placed the stones on her body. He then went and bought some laudanum to kill himself but he did not succeed. He begged everyone concerned to forgive him for what he had done.

Burton's hanging took place at eight o'clock on the morning of 6 August 1883 but the story did not end there. William Marwood was the executioner appointed to hang Burton. Marwood arrived at Durham on Saturday afternoon and reported to the prison to inspect the scaffold. The High Sheriff offered him accommodation within the prison 'lest some of the invincibles should take advantage of the opportunity to remove him'. Marwood declined the proffered protection and instead went to the *Dun Cow Inn* where he had stayed in the past.

On the morning of the execution James was led to the scaffold and Marwood secured the rope. As the drop fell the rope became entangled with the condemned man's left arm and seemed to slip up to his chin, Marwood had to jerk him quickly out of the pit. Blood could be seen coming from James' mouth and nose, his neck was broken but he was still alive and in great pain. He was placed on a seat beside the scaffold between two warders whilst Marwood disentangled the rope. Once satisfied that the rope was now properly in place, Marwood jerked James back into the pit with such force that the prisoner was carried right across the cavity. As the body swung back, Marwood

Sign for the Dun Cow Inn *where William Marwood stayed.* Author's collection

caught hold of the rope and gave it two or three jerks. James Burton's pain ended as death eventually took him.

An inquest was held into the way the execution had been handled and Marwood was exonerated of blame. The local press and witnesses were not so ready to excuse the man who had once been a shoemaker and had been carrying out executions for the past eleven years. It was suggested that Marwood was drunk, which he denied. He said the rope had not actually slipped but that Burton had fainted and fallen back; in falling his elbow had caught in the slack of the rope just as the lever was pulled. The press also accused Marwood of parading the streets of Durham like a victorious army general and stated that he should have stayed within the prison, not at a public inn. Marwood said there was no accommodation available to him within the prison and denied parading the streets of Durham. The executioner accused the press of lying and he stated he had never bungled an execution. I wonder if James Burton would have agreed with Marwood?

Shortly afterwards on 4 September 1883, Marwood met his own death when he succumbed to inflammation of the lungs.

Seaham Harbour: 1900

Isabella Bowes had spent years eking out a living for her family by collecting and selling sea coal. Isabella's husband, John Bowes, did not work and often ill-treated his wife and family. On 21 August, Bowes threatened his wife and daughter with a kicking. Isabella decided she had had enough and left the house taking her daughter with her. She took out a summons against her husband and applied for a separation order. On Saturday morning 8 September, Isabella went as usual to the beach to collect coal. She was near the Ballast Tips when her husband approached. Isabella's young nephew, Proctor, Isabella's daughter and a number of women were on the beach at the time and all heard the exchange between the estranged couple.

Isabella was picking up coals and had started to walk up the bank. Bowes said he would collect more coals for her, but she replied that she wanted nothing more to do with him. As Isabella bent down to collect another coal, the witnesses saw

Seaham harbour. Author's collection

Bowes pick up a four-foot long piece of wood that was lying nearby and strike his wife on the head with it. She fell to the ground and he struck her again three times. He then threw the wood down and walked a short distance away. Turning round, Bowes headed back to his wife and taking a cloth from his pocket he wet it in the sea and lifting her head commenced bathing Isabella's face.

One of the women had gone for the police and when they arrived Bowes was holding his wife's head, kissing her and asking her to speak to him. If the first blow had not killed her, then certainly one of the following blows had. Asked why he had killed her, Bowes said she had aggravated him sorely and he had hit her in a fit of passion.

John Bowes was tried before Justice Grantham and sentenced to death for wilful murder. James Billington performed the execution on 12 December as the first year of the new century was drawing to an end.

Sunderland: 1903

James Duffy had been living with Ellen Newman for just over a year. Duffy was a widower with a grown family and Ellen had left her husband. The youngest of Duffy's children, a boy of fourteen, lived with them. The couple were heavy drinkers and Ellen supported Duffy with money from immoral earnings. The two were known by the neighbours to be constantly quarrelling. It was also known that Duffy sometimes abused Ellen, so it was no great surprise when their last argument ended in tragedy.

One Sunday afternoon in September, Duffy walked into the central police station in Sunderland and declared that he had strangled his wife. Although he was not drunk, he had been drinking. The police asked him when and where he had committed the crime and he answered that he had killed her that morning at 4 Back Durham Street. A constable went to the address, which was a house that let rooms, and found Ellen lying on the bed fully dressed and quite dead. She had, as Duffy said, been strangled.

Almost a year previously, when their relationship was quite new, the pair quarreled bitterly. Duffy had tried to cut Ellen's throat and then his own. He had been sentenced to one month's imprisonment at the time. When he was released, Duffy went back to live with Ellen and had not worked since. Duffy, even at his trial, never came forward with any reason for the killing other than it was a row about money and 'he could not stand any more'.

He was found guilty of the wilful murder of his paramour and was sentenced to death by Justice Grantham. On 8 December 1903, William and John Billington carried out the hanging.

Seaham Harbour: 1904

A man walked into the County Police Barracks at Durham on the morning of 6 July with a long written statement confessing to a murder. On being questioned the man said his name was George Breeze and he had murdered a woman named Margaret Jane Chisholm. PC Trueman was sent to investigate and was directed to a house in Back Church Street at Dawdon near Seaham Harbour. On receiving no reply to his knock, he entered the premises and found a woman in bed apparently asleep. Beside the bed was a young child slapping the woman's hands apparently trying to awaken her. On closer inspection the PC realised the woman was dead.

Margaret had been married for three years. The house where she was found only had one room and she, her husband, their two-year-old child and a lodger, George Breeze, all slept in that room. Margaret's husband and their lodger both worked as miners at New Seaham Colliery and were also well known footballers.

According to Breeze's statement on that fateful morning, Margaret's husband had gone to work leaving him on the couch. Breeze had strangled Margaret,

In a fit of mad passion driven by her handsome face. She had made him do what God had ordained no man to do.

Margaret had told him that morning that her husband had told her that he was jealous of her and Breeze and she wished she were dead. Breeze had then asked her if there would be any harm in him killing her and she had replied that she did not care. He then added,

I then strangled her. I am sorry for her. I would not have done it

if I had thought of the seriousness of it. I was ready to go to the scaffold taking three steps at a time, and also put the rope around my own neck, because I knew that we were both to meet where there was plenty, and none would laugh and jeer at you.

Breeze stood trial before Justice Grantham and asked if he had anything to say. He pleaded guilty and refused to be defended saying he was not sorry as it was no good being sorry once the thing was done.

When Justice Grantham sentenced the prisoner to death, Breeze said 'Thank you very much, I hope there will be no reprieve'.

George Breeze was twenty-one-years old when he was hanged for the murder of Margaret Chisholm on 2 August 1904. William Billington was the executioner assisted by John Ellis.

Hamsterly: 1908

Matthew James Dodds, who was forty-three, and his wife, Mary Jane, were supposed to be respectable people. In fact, when Mary was found dead the local newspaper printed that they were 'well respected in the neighbourhood as Dodds was a member of the Nonconformist Church and Mary had private means'. The real story was that amongst their nearest

Hamsterly Village. Durham Federation of Women's Institutes and Countryside Books

The Cross Keys *at Bishop Auckland, a public house from 1881.* Author's collection

neighbours it was common knowledge that they had a stormy
relationship. Dodds had been heard to use threats against his
wife. He later said this was because his wife had a drink
problem. On 20 February 1908 Dodds claimed he had been
working in his father's joinery shop until four in the afternoon.
When he returned home he found his wife lying dead upon the
fire hearth, badly burnt. Dodds went for a neighbour, Sarah
Wade, telling her his wife had burnt to death. On Sarah entering
the house she found Mary with her clothes still alight but there
was no fire in the grate. It was assumed that Mary had fallen and

had been burnt to death. In one of her hands was grasped a burnt out cinder. A coroner's inquest was carried out and the death was stated to be an accident.

Stories and rumours began to circulate and the coroner's suspicions were aroused. He gave an order on 9 March at Bishop Auckland police court for Mary's body to be exhumed. This was done the following day. Three doctors carried out a postmortem and were all in agreement that death had been caused by strangulation. They could not tell whether the burns to the body had been inflicted before or after death. Evidence pointed to Mary's own shawl having been used to strangle her. Dodds was arrested for the murder of his wife.

At the trial neighbours gave evidence saying they had heard shouting coming from the Dodds' house from around two-thirty that day. The noise had gone on for some considerable time but none of the neighbours had interfered as quarrelling between the couple was often heard. Alice Dowson Stephenson, landlady of the *Cross Keys*, stated that the couple had been frequent visitors to her establishment and were always quarrelling. She had once seen Dodds kick Mary from the archway of the gate to the footpath. Other witnesses had seen Dodds hit his wife with a sweeping brush and heard him threaten to 'make her into mincemeat'. It was also stated that Mary often had bruises, cuts

Witton Road, Hamsterley. Author's collection

and black eyes. Joseph Jopling Brown, a medical student, had taken a will written by Mary and left in his keeping to Dodds' house the day after the funeral. Before Brown could read it, Dodds produced another will dated January 1908 leaving all Mary's money and goods to him absolutely.

Dodds insisted he had not been in the house at the time of his wife's death but could not explain how shouting was heard. The prosecution believed a quarrel had broken out between them, Dodds had lost his temper, strangled Mary Jane and then tried to dump her in the fire. She had probably grasped the cinder in the agony of her death throes. It was also believed that she might have been forced by Dodds to write the second will but that could not be proved. When the jury brought in a verdict of guilty, Justice Grantham said no other conclusion could possibly have been reached. He sentenced Dodds to death with no recommendation for mercy. Henry and Thomas Pierrepoint carried out the execution on 8 August 1908.

Chapter 20

The Suffering of the Innocents

Durham, 1819

George Atcheson, who was sixty-eight, stood trial for 'rape on the body of Isabella Ramshaw, a child under ten years of age'.

Atcheson was found guilty and sentenced to be hanged. From the time of his arrest to his last seconds on the scaffold on 12 April he was repentant. He expressed a wish that his untimely end would serve as a deterrent to others from carrying out the crime.

Shildon: 1866

An inquest was held at the *Fox and Hounds* public house in Shildon on the body of a newborn female child. On 14 May Christiana Jefferson, who was separated from her husband and lived in Middridge, had gone to William Bousfield who was the sexton at Shildon. She had the body of a child in a box saying that the birth had taken place two days before but she had been at work so could not bring the body sooner. Bousfield asked

Fox and Hounds, *Shildon*. The author

546

whose baby it was but Christiana would not tell him. Without opening the box, the sexton buried it in the churchyard. A police constable, Robert Harrison, upon hearing about the event, went to the Jefferson's house. Christiana's daughter, Esther, eventually admitted that the child was hers but insisted that it had been stillborn. Christiana then offered the constable a coin to keep quiet about the affair. Harrison refused and went to the deputy coroner. On 29 May it was ordered that the body be exhumed. The baby was then handed to Samuel Fielden, a surgeon to perform a post-mortem. Fielden stated at the inquest that he had attended Esther a few months before and had suspected she was pregnant. Both mother and daughter denied it. He again attended her on 11 May when she still denied being pregnant. Fielden was called out to see Esther again on 12 May but he did not go. His postmortem on the child's body showed that it was full term but he could not say for certain whether she had been born alive. There were no marks of external violence on the body so he could not say why death had taken place.

Dinah Rycroft, a neighbour, had been called to the Jefferson's house on the morning of 11 May. Christiana said Esther was very ill. Dinah told her that she thought Esther was in labour. This was denied adamantly. The following day Dinah went again to see how Esther was. She seemed better but nothing was said about her having given birth.

Elizabeth Jefferson, Esther's sister, had gone to the house on 11 May. Esther was very ill but although she was stouter there was no suspicion of pregnancy. By the time night came, Esther was worse and at about three in the morning Elizabeth sent for Dr Fielden but he did not attend. Eventually, Christiana delivered Esther of a female child. The baby breathed at first and Christiana took it to wash. The next time Elizabeth looked the baby was on the dresser and appeared to be dead. She then went to Dr Fielden and told him his services were no longer required but did not say anything about the birth. Elizabeth stated that she did not believe anyone did any harm to the child. She felt it had been a difficult and protracted birth and that was why the baby died. When all the witnesses had spoken the jury retired. After an absence of about fifteen minutes they returned an open verdict.

A typical working class family's house at Shildon.
Author's collection

Sunnybrow: 1900

Samuel Price was a forty-six year old miner. He had three daughters living with him, Catherine, Susannah and Jane. His son, who was sixteen, had left home. Price's wife had died when their youngest daughter, Catherine, was three months old.

On 25 August, Catherine, who was by this time twenty months old, took ill and on 27 August a doctor was called in. The doctor told Price that the child had an ulcerated mouth and stomach and in his opinion Catherine was undernourished. Proper food and milk was prescribed and the doctor left. The child was left in the eldest daughter, Jane's care.

On 13 September, Jane left home. She, like her brother, had had enough of her father's drunken habits. Jane had asked her father for money to buy food for Catherine but he refused. After Jane left, Price gave Susannah money to buy two pints of milk and some port wine for the baby. By this time Catherine was seriously ill and she died on 18 September.

Catherine's death was due to bronchitis and pneumonia brought on by the fact that she was weak from undernourishment and was only half the weight she should have been. Samuel Price was charged with manslaughter. Price said the child had always been sickly and he had not thought she would live anyway. He said he had never refused money to Jane. Both his daughters could go to Mr Elliott's shop at Willington and get groceries on credit. Milk was in short supply but he bought it when he could.

Susannah backed up Jane's story and said she had heard her father refuse money to buy food for the baby. Both daughters stated their father ignored Catherine and acted as if she was not there. Samuel Ragg, a friend of Price's, stated that he had helped Price home on 16 September because he was so drunk. When Ragg saw the little girl he had said to Price that the child was dying. Price said 'it would have to take its chance whether it lived or not'. He then ordered Ragg out of the house.

The jury found Price guilty of manslaughter with extenuating circumstances. Justice Grantham sentenced him to six month's imprisonment.

West Stanley: 1908

Jeremiah O'Connor was a miner at the Stanley pit. The fifty-five year old man had been lodging, along with another man, Michael Brown, in Pool Street, West Stanley for more than three years. The little house was the home of Thomas Donnelly, his wife and two children, a boy and a girl. The two lodgers slept in the same room as the children. Mary, who was ten, had formed a close friendship with O'Connor.

It was Monday, 14 December and O'Connor had been on a drinking binge for a few days. When he returned home that evening the little girl set off with O'Connor for a walk in the country. Neither of the two of them came home that night. A detailed search of the surrounding area was organised. On Thursday, four miles from West Stanley, at Gibside, a stranger was noticed acting rather oddly. A man had called at the cottage of Mrs Boyd on the eastern side of Gibside. He was trembling all over and could hardly eat the food that Mrs Boyd gave him. The story the man mumbled was that a navvy had attacked him, stolen his money and taken his little lass away. After showing Mrs Boyd his blood soaked shirt sleeve and several cuts on his arm he left. Returning the following day the man told Mrs Boyd that he had slept outside all night. Mrs Boyd told him that she was going to tell his story to the police, whereupon, the strange man ran off. The police were informed and the description given to them by Mrs Boyd matched the description of O'Connor. More searchers were called in, swelling the number to more than one hundred. Nearly a week after her disappearance, on Sunday 20 December, Mary's body was eventually found under a hedge on a field at Pea Farm, which was situated a few miles from her home.

The horribly mutilated body gave witness to the fact that the little girl had died a terrible death. Mary had been brutally sexually assaulted and then violently attacked with a sharp instrument, probably a knife. The injuries were so severe that she had been almost disemboweled. Dr Benson, who examined the body, thought Mary had been dead about a week, probably since the night she went missing.

O'Connor was arrested by Inspector Stark on Saturday morning near the village of Tonfield. When the Inspector told him he had a warrant for his arrest, O'Connor collapsed and had to be taken to a nearby farmhouse until he recovered. He was then driven by pony and trap to Consett. The police felt it would be unwise to take their prisoner anywhere near Stanley because, understandably, emotions were running so high. When questioned, O'Connor repeated the story that he had told Mrs Boyd. He said that a navvy who had stolen his money and taken Mary had inflicted the wounds on his arm when O'Connor had tried to fight him off.

At the ensuing trial before Justice Lawrence, the prisoner maintained his innocence and repeated his previous story. Mr Lowenthal, for the prosecution, said that O'Connor had raped the child, killed her and then inflicted the wounds upon himself. If the story about the navvy were true, then why had O'Connor not gone straight to the police? The jury found O'Connor guilty and he was sentenced to death.

O'Connor, originally from Ireland, had two daughters and a son living in Haswell where he had stayed before moving to West Stanley. He had served in the Royal Irish Fusiliers and the Durham Militia. While in prison, O'Connor only received one visit and that was from one of his daughters and his son. He did not take advantage of the new law of appeal and neither did anyone appeal to the Home Secretary on his behalf for clemency. It was recorded that O'Connor spoke not a word and faced the gallows with resignation. Henry Pierrepoint, who was assisted by his older brother, Thomas, carried out the execution on 23 February 1909.

Had Jeremiah O'Connor, who had been a friend to Mary Donnelly for three years suddenly turned into a monster and raped and murdered the little girl? Or was his story of a navvy true? Only O'Connor, and perhaps one other, knew the truth.

Henry Pierrepoint, executioner from 1901-10 and Thomas Pierrepoint, executioner from 1906-46. Author's collection

Chapter 21

Attacked with a Poker
1874

The scene of this terrible tragedy was High Bush Blade, a short distance from Dipton, which is about three miles from Consett. Dipton was an extensive colliery village housing a large number of Irish families. At the time, High Bush Blade consisted of four houses. In one lived an Irish miner, Phillip Burdy, his family and his brother, Simon. A short distance away was Hill Top where another Irish miner, Hugh Daley, and his family lived.

Saturday drinking sessions often ended in brawls between the workers. They had their wages and after a week of unpleasant toil in the mines, they were ready for a good drink and to let off steam. This Saturday evening in November was no exception. Daley had staggered home intoxicated and after having something to eat, was helped into bed by his wife and a neighbour, Ann Smith. Another neighbour, John Power was also in the Daley's house at this time. A few minutes later Phillip Burdy entered the house. Suddenly Daley jumped out of bed, went across to the fireplace and picked up the heavy, iron poker. When Burdy saw this, he ran outside but Daley followed him looking like a madman, half dressed and wielding the poker. He caught up with Burdy and dealt him a violent blow to the head with the poker. Power, who had witnessed what had taken place, ran to fetch Simon Burdy. The injured man staggered into a nearby house where the occupant, Mrs Smith, dressed the wound to his head.

Burdy had left his cap in Daley's house, so a little later he returned there to retrieve it. Perhaps he thought Daley would have calmed down or been asleep by then. As soon as he entered, Daley jumped from the bed and attacked Burdy again and began reigning blows on his head. Burdy ran outside but could not get away from his attacker. There were three other men present in the house at this time but none interfered. They later stated they were too frightened of Daley's violent character. Someone went for assistance from the police. PC Forster was about a mile away from the scene and ran there as fast as he was able. While still a little distance from the house he could hear the noise of the blows being delivered by the poker. When PC Forster entered the house, Daley threatened to strike him also and yelled that he would kill him too. Daley had hold of the poker with both hands and aimed to strike the PC with it but he slipped and fell. The PC quickly pounced on Daley and handcuffed him.

Burdy was carried back into Daley's house and Dr Hunter of Stebbhouse was summoned. His face and head almost unrecognizable as a human being, Burdy died soon after the doctor arrived.

Daley was known as a drunken, idle, violent man of dour countenance. Burdy, on the other hand, although he took a drink, was well thought of in the community by his workmates. What puzzled everyone concerned was a reason for the attack. The two men had been on friendly terms until then. The reason was never forthcoming. Daley would not say and Burdy could not.

An inquest took place at the *Prince of Wales* at Flinthill in Dipton and Daley was committed for trial at the Durham Assizes. With all the witnesses that had been present during the attack, the jury did not find it hard to convict Daley of murder. The judge, Baron Cleasby, pronounced the death sentence. William Marwood carried out the hanging on 28 December 1874.

Chapter 22

Manslaughter at South Church
1878

Sarah Cooper was married to George Cooper, an ironworker and they had one child. In 1872 the couple parted and Sarah went to live with Joseph Nicholson. She became known as Sarah Nicholson and had two children to Joseph. The couple and the three children went to live in Coundon in October 1877. Joseph was known as a lazy, good-for-nothing who would not work and ill-treated Sarah and the children. The neighbours often heard shouting, screaming and crying coming from the Nicholson's house. Sometimes, at night, Sarah would take refuge from Joseph's violence in a neighbour's house. The family was almost starving, the children undernourished and poorly clad. While living in Coundon, Sarah began hawking to earn some money. She would take a pony and cart and sell her wares from door to door. The little Sarah earned must have been handed to Joseph because at night she would beg food for herself and the children. In 1878 the family moved to Adamson's Row in South Church, near Bishop Auckland. Again the neighbours saw and heard the violence within the family.

Inevitably the violence ended with dire consequences. On Wednesday 22 May Sarah left the house at nine in the morning to hawk her wares. She had told Joseph she would return about one o'clock. When Sarah had not returned by one-thirty Joseph became agitated. Three times he went to the village to look for her and then went to a neighbour, Esther Hind, saying he had no 'meat' or 'baccy' until Sarah returned. Mrs Hind told Joseph that Sarah must be busy selling and to be patient to which Joseph replied that 'he would give her something when she comes'. Joseph then returned to his house and in his temper kicked Sarah's seven-year old daughter.

Mrs Hind afterwards related what took place when Sarah

eventually returned at about three that afternoon. The little girl, who because of undernourishment was tiny for her age, ran to her mother showing her the marks of Joseph's attack. Sarah became angry and shouted at Joseph who retaliated by hitting her hard across the face with the flat of his hand. Sarah took a sand stone from her cart and threatened to hit Joseph with it if he touched her or her child again. Joseph hit her again on the other side of her face so Sarah threw the stone and kicked her attacker with her clog. At this, Joseph's rage became uncontrollable, he ran at Sarah and using his full weight he punched her in the chest just under the left breast. She dropped to the ground like a stone. Looking up at Joseph she said 'Oh Joe, you've done it at last' and then she became still. Mrs Hind and another neighbour, Margaret Blackburn, who had witnessed the events, ran to assist Sarah. They carried her into Mrs Hind's house but within minutes Sarah was dead.

Joseph was arrested and an inquest heard at Musgrave's *Blue Bells Inn* at South Church. Seemingly remorseful and crying bitterly throughout the inquest, he denied intending to kill Sarah. Joseph stated that she had a history of heart trouble. The post-mortem showed, in the surgeon's opinion, it was the blow to the chest coupled with her heart not being very strong that had caused Sarah's death. The surgeon also added that although there was heart disease it was minor and Sarah could have lived with it for many years.

At Joseph's trial at the Durham Assizes on a charge of manslaughter, the jury decided the death was not caused with intent. Although they found him guilty it was with a strong recommendation for mercy. He was given a sentence of twelve months hard labour.

Sarah's daughter at the age of seven was so small, it was stated by the aunt who took her in that she could fit into a one-year old child's clothes.

Chapter 23

Murder Aboard the 'William Leckie' 1878

Sunderland Docks was thriving and prosperous in the nineteenth century. As well as the revenue generated by the cargoes that were shipped to and from the town, there was also the spending by the ships' crews. Having been at sea for long periods of time, when a port was reached the crew would be ready for some relaxation. In the main these men would just have a good time with wine, woman and song. On occasion, however, too much of a good thing, namely alcohol, would cause a brooding resentment and anger against a fellow man. Skirmishes, quarrels and drunken brawls would take place, sometimes with fatal results.

In June of 1878 the barque *William Leckie* was at anchor in Sunderland Roads. The vessel belonged to Mr William Nicholson and other gentlemen from the town. It was preparing

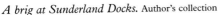

A brig at Sunderland Docks. Author's collection

to sail to Montevideo with a cargo of coal. The master of the vessel was Captain Lumley Fletcher and he had engaged thirty-two year old Robert Vest as cook and ship's steward. Vest had previously been unemployed for some time.

On 26 June Captain Fletcher went to Newcastle on an early morning train to procure the necessary papers for his vessel. He arrived back to board the barque at about four in the afternoon intending to weigh anchor and set sail but there was insufficient wind. While on board the captain noticed that Vest was drunk. He checked the seals on the stores but they were secure. Vest, therefore, must have brought alcohol on board from ashore. Captain Fletcher told Vest that he would not tolerate drunkenness aboard his ship and he was to leave his duties and do no more until the morning. Fletcher then threatened Vest that he would 'have to go forward' meaning he would be reduced to the ranks of a common seaman. John Wallace was an old trusted pilot aboard the vessel and as such was in charge when the captain was absent. The pilot was known as a peaceful, inoffensive man who only interfered officiously with the crew if it was absolutely necessary. It seems that Wallace had already spoken to Vest about the state he was in. It is not known whether Wallace actually reported Vest's condition to the captain. It was, however, certain that the captain and Wallace both supported each other on this type of complaint. The events that followed the reprimand show that Vest must have been very angry and, unbeknown to them, was harbouring a grudge against his employers.

To pass the time until the barque could set sail, three of the crewmen, an apprentice named Thomas William Talbot and seamen Richard Smith and John Moss, were on the forward deck with a concertina and a violin. The boatswain and carpenter were aft near the main rigging. They were all suddenly startled by a shout for help that came from the water closet. They ran towards it to find Vest holding Wallace by the collar and threatening him with a large bowie knife. Talbot tried to strike the arm Vest was holding the knife with to make him release it but to no avail. The apprentice then ran to the rail for a belaying pin, but could not get one out. Before anyone could stop him Vest ploughed the knife deep into Wallace's stomach.

Colliers loading at Shields in 1844 by T H Hair. Durham Mining Museum

The large knife disappeared to its hilt. Wallace had been using the toilet at the time of the attack so he was in a state of undress. He staggered up pulling the knife free as he did so, then dropped to his knees at the door of the closet. Wallace then fell back insensible. Because his clothes were not fastened the wound was

Long months at sea meant that feeding the crew adequately was important for the morale of the ship. This is the galley of the Trincomalee, *an 1817 frigate, which has been restored and is berthed within the Hartlepool Quay.* John C Harrison

in full view. It was so deep that the man's bowels were protruding. There was also a gash on Wallace's throat where Vest must have stabbed him before he could shout for help. Another apprentice, George Dodds, that was there asked Vest what he deserved for stabbing an old man but Vest did not reply. By this time the captain had arrived and ordered bandages for Wallace's wounds and brandy. Before these were obtained the old pilot had died.

Vest was lashed to the deck and word was sent ashore.

Sergeant Lakin and other officers arrived on the tug *Champion*. Vest was taken into custody and removed to the Low Street police station.

At the inquest, held at Sunderland police courts, Vest said that the captain had threatened him and that Wallace had pushed him about. He also said that he had asked to be put ashore and the captain had refused. Captain Fletcher denied these accusations, except for the threat of demoting Vest because he was so drunk he was not capable of carrying out the rest of his duties that day. After reprimanding Vest, the captain had ordered a keg of rum to be opened and everyone aboard was given one glass each, except for Vest because he had already had enough to drink. This would probably have fuelled Vest's anger and need for revenge. It was thought that if Captain Fletcher had been found instead of Wallace it would have been him that would have suffered Vest's fury.

The heads (water closet or toilet) for use by the captain would have been enclosed for privacy. This is a view of the heads for the use of the crew on the Trincomalee, *an 1817 frigate, which has been restored and is berthed within the Hartlepool Quay.* Author's collection

At the Durham Assizes presided over by Judge Baggalley, on investigation of Vest's character it was found that he had been incarcerated previously for assaulting Mr White, the Seaham gas manager. Witnesses came forward with statements about his violent temper. Vest had been known to brandish knives in a threatening manner. It was also found that he had resigned from a good situation because he felt that his employers were exploiting the working classes to make their fortunes. He had decided to write a book on the subject saying that he would make a fortune and gain his independency by selling his story at 2s 6d (15p) a copy. Because people laughed at this idea, in a frenzy he tore the manuscript into bits. Vest had also made a very strange statement:

> *When a soldier, I, in duty to my country killed and slayed many innocent beings who never did me the slightest injury; then why cannot I kill my enemies, which I will do and be hanged for it.*

No one except Vest, Captain Fletcher and Wallace knew exactly what was said and done during the altercation aboard ship. The fact remained that Vest had taken an old man's life and he was found guilty of Wallace's murder and sentenced to death. His execution was carried out on 30 July 1878 by William Marwood.

Chapter 24

Long Awaited Justice
1882

In Sunderland on Saturday 26 February 1869 a woman of about forty years of age, Maria Fitzimmons, was found dead on the floor of her bedroom. She had died of multiple stab wounds to the region of her heart, inflicted by a thin, sharp instrument, probably a knife. The room in which she was found was on the first floor of a house in Baine's Lane, where rooms were let out. The house was in a terrible condition and the room in which Maria lived could only be described as wretched. The furniture consisted of a dilapidated bed, two chairs and a rickety table.

An initial inquest was held at the *Butcher's Arms* in Coronation Street, Sunderland. Dorothy Wilkinson lived in a house almost opposite Maria and had known her for a few years. Maria had gone into Dorothy's house on the Saturday afternoon. She had been 'stupid drunk' and a few minutes after she arrived a man had followed her in. Dorothy had never seen the man before but said she would be able to recognise him and that he looked like a sailor. The man had kept asking Maria for his coat and stockings and he said that if she returned them he would not ask for his money back. Dorothy did not know what money he was talking about. The pair began to kiss and then left arm in arm to go to Maria's room. Other witnesses that had seen the man with Maria all agreed on his mode of dress and that he was probably a sailor. A reward of £100 was offered for information leading to the arrest of the murderer. Although the police questioned many people and the murder was well publicised in the local press, nobody was arrested in connection with the crime at that time.

On 27 March the body of a man was found in Hartlepool harbour. The man had been in the water for some weeks and was badly decomposed. By his height, the colour of his hair and what clothing could still be recognised it was thought that this might be Maria's murderer. Although the man was never identified it

A map showing the area of Coronation Street Author's collection

was later ascertained that he was not the man the police were looking for.

In April of 1869 Peter Conner was arrested in Wapping accused of Maria's murder. Conner's clothes and his personal appearance fitted the description that had been given by witnesses. Conner protested his innocence saying he had never even been to Sunderland. One of the witnesses agreed to travel to Wapping to identify the prisoner as being the man seen with Maria. Conner was not the man and after being in custody for a week was released. Conner asked if he could have compensation for losing a week's wages but was told there was no money in the fund to give him.

Eventually in April of 1882, the perpetrator was brought to justice through his own confession.

Thomas Fury alias Thomas Wright alias Charles H Cort, was serving a fifteen year sentence of penal servitude in Pentonville Prison at the time of his confession. Perhaps he felt that the noose was preferable to the conditions of his incarceration within the prison. Fury was a well-read, intelligent man so maybe found life in confinement harder to cope with than some might have done.

At the beginning of Fury's trial, he pleaded guilty. Justice Williams explained to him that little reliance could be placed upon a confession uncorroborated by other evidence and asked him to reconsider his plea. Fury thought for a moment and after thanking Justice Williams changed his plea to 'not guilty.'

As the trial commenced the story that began thirteen years previously began to unfold through the testimony of witnesses. The first to be called was William Lawrence, now working at Bolckow's steelworks at Eston, but in 1869 he had been a seaman. A bottle schooner, the *Lollard* had been lying at Sunderland. The crew consisted of himself, the master and mate and two able seamen, one of whom he had known as Tom, or Thomas Wright. On 19 February Lawrence and the man he knew as Wright had gone ashore. Wright was dressed in fustian trousers, guernsey and a reefer jacket. As they walked up the High Street, Wright had entered a shop and come out with two sharp pointed knives, one of which he gave to Lawrence. They went to the *Wear Music Hall* and then to a public house near

Baines Lane. Lawrence then went back to his ship leaving Wright ashore. Wright returned to the ship at about seven o'clock the following evening, smelling strongly of drink and with his face scratched and his finger cut. He said he had been drugged and lost his money. When Lawrence went ashore that night he heard about the murder of Maria Fitzsimmons. It was suspected by the police that a seaman could have committed the crime but the ship was still allowed to sail a few days later. When the ship docked at its next port, which was London, Wright deserted taking with him some clothes and a pocketbook belonging to Lawrence. The pocketbook was produced in court, having been found in the Serpentine River, along with newspaper cuttings relating to the murder.

James Harris had been a policeman in London 1869 and had spoken to a man that looked like Fury in Fleet Street. At the time the man had tried to incriminate another man who was aboard the *Lollard*. Harris took notes at the time and these were produced in the court. The man made an appointment to meet Harris the next day with further information. Harris then told him that the police believed the murderer had sailed with a ship to London. Of course, the following day's appointment was never kept.

The next witness was a clockmaker, James Gilhonley, the witness that had travelled to Wapping in 1869. On the night the murder took place Gilhonley had been drinking in Frank Duggan's beerhouse in Baines Lane. He had known the murdered girl, who he described as 'an unfortunate' and sat and spoke to her for a while. She was in the company of a man dressed in the clothes Lawrence had described that the man he knew as Wright was wearing that night.

Margaret Lafferty had lived next door to Maria Fitzsimmons and on that fateful night she had heard Maria cry out. On entering the house to see what was wrong, Maria was standing at the top of the stairs crying that 'the man was going to murder her'. A man was putting on a jacket that fitted the description the other witnesses had given. Mrs Lafferty told him to go and he replied that the girl had stolen 15s (75p) from him. Mrs Lafferty left and a little while later Maria came to her still saying the man was going to kill her. The two women entered the house where the man was sitting on a stool. Mrs Lafferty noticed that

Maria's boots were on the fire. On this been pointed out Maria started abusing the man. He became very angry and said if she spoke another word he would stab her. Mrs Lafferty and Maria left. That night Mrs Lafferty saw the pair enter Maria's house together. A little later Mrs Lafferty became worried and went to see if the girl was okay, she found Maria's body lying on the bedroom floor.

A man giving the name of Charles Henry Cort was arrested in August 1879 and sentenced to fifteen years penal servitude for an unrelated crime. He was taken to Pentonville in October 1881. Since the day of his admission to the prison he had been on report four times for not carrying out his allotted tasks. (No doubt punishment would have been severe). Early in 1882 Cort wrote on his slate that his real name was Thomas Fury and a full confession to the murder of Maria Fitzsimmons. In March his confession was repeated verbally to a prison director after which he was transferred to Durham to stand trial.

Although they all thought there was a similarity, not one of the witnesses could swear that the prisoner in the dock was the same man in the events they had described as happening thirteen years previously. In the summing up of the case, the judge suggested that the jury would have to decide whether this was a false confession so that Fury could commit legal suicide rather than suffer imprisonment or whether the facts showed him to really be the guilty party. The jury found him guilty. They felt there were many facts in his confession that only the murderer could have known and because of the links the witnesses had provided in the chain of events surrounding the murder.

Justice was a long time in coming for Maria but come it did when William Marwood hanged Thomas Fury at Durham on 16 May 1882.

Chapter 25

Sibling Rivalry
1883

We can choose our friends but not our families and rivalry and anger among siblings is quite common. In this case the results of anger went to the extreme and ended in catastrophe.

The Robinson family had a two-roomed cottage at Stanhope where they had a small farm called Holling Hill. The family consisted of Matilda Robinson, her four sons, Ralph, Thomas, Bainbridge and George and a daughter who was considered 'weak minded.' Ralph was the eldest son but because he was crippled with a useless left arm and a thigh that was severely out of joint, could only manage small jobs around the farm. Thomas and George were lead miners and could not live at home as the mines they worked at were too far away. When Thomas did come home he often 'chaffed' Ralph about his work around the farm. On Sunday, 3 June, Ralph, Thomas and George sat down to their meal at about twelve thirty. Their mother was pottering about the cottage and they were all discussing family matters. Matilda mentioned the mines that might be opened nearby but said that if Thomas and Ralph both had to live together in the cottage she would quietly go to Stanhope Workhouse. An argument then started between Ralph and Thomas about work on the farm. Thomas accused Ralph of writing letters about him. Suddenly Ralph jumped up from his seat, lent towards Thomas and with the knife he had been using to cut his food stabbed his brother in the heart. The wounded man rose from his seat and staggered towards the door but fell before he reached it. George pinned Ralph's arms and shouted for Bainbridge to take the knife from Ralph's hand. As this was done, George kept hold of his brother and sent Bainbridge for a doctor and the police. George then went to Thomas who was lying face down on the stone slabs. He turned his brother over

Market Place, Stanhope. Author's collection

and saw that his waistcoat was saturated with blood and he was dead.

It transpired that Thomas thought Ralph had written a letter to a prospective employer belittling his character. The rest of the family did not know if this were true but agreed that the two brothers had never seen eye to eye and were always arguing with each other. A few months before this terrible deed took place Ralph, not being very steady on his feet, had fallen and banged the back of his head. Matilda said that her son had been very edgy and bad tempered since the fall. Ralph had also had a bad attack of smallpox from which he had not been expected to recover.

PC Sedgewick arrested Ralph and as he was being led away the prisoner said to the PC 'I have had an awful bad time with him you know.' Ralph also turned to his family and said 'I bid you all farewell friends and hope he'll go to hell.'

At the trial Ralph was found guilty of manslaughter. The jury had taken a lenient view because it was a dinner knife that had been used in a fit of anger and not a premeditated crime. Also they felt that Ralph had not had an easy life. The judge summed up by saying that there had been enough evidence for a verdict of guilty to wilful murder but that the jury had been merciful. He then sentenced Ralph Robinson to twenty years penal servitude.

Chapter 26

The Blackleg
1883

In 1882 there was a strike at Ushaw Moor Colliery in Durham. Thomas Pyle was known as a blackleg for working as a platelayer at the colliery while the strike was in place. There was always a lot of ill feeling amongst the other miners against these blacklegs and Pyle was on the receiving end of his co-workers scorn.

On the morning of 2 April 1882, Pyle's body was discovered in the hedge side at Prior's Path. This was near the gateway that opened into the high ground of the Catholic Cemetery. He was lying face down and on being turned over a large gash to the lower part of his face could be seen. He had apparently met his death by a nail being driven into his throat. Nearby was a fence rail that contained nails.

The previous evening had been a Saturday, so the inns would have been full of working men enjoying some relaxation. The police interviewed everyone who may have passed along Prior's Path on their way home that night. Much later, when no one had been arrested for the crime, bills were posted offering a £200 reward for the conviction of the murderer.

Nearly sixteen months later Peter Bray was arrested. He had been in the hands of the police many times. At one time he had served seven years penal servitude and been given twenty-five strokes of the cat's tail. The offence had been a robbery with violence at Crossgate Peth. When the police made the arrest in 1883 in connection with the murder of Thomas Pyle, Bray was just leaving Durham gaol after completing a sentence for another offence. He had intended to rejoin the Hartlepool Militia in which he had previously served.

During Bray's trial at the Durham Assizes, four miners, who had all resided at Bear Park with Bray at the time of the murder, came forward as witnesses. Two of the miners were brothers,

A part of Durham Castle. Author's collection

George and James Race. One by one they gave their evidence blaming Bray for the crime. They all agreed that Bray had said he would kill Pyle for being a blackleg. On the night in question, as they had all walked home along Prior's Path, they had seen Pyle lying by the hedge drunk. A man, whom they did not know, had stood over him offering assistance, but Pyle had been too drunk to rise. Bray had come up to the miners and asked who it was that was lying drunk. When they told him it was Pyle he had said 'let's away back and kill the b......'. The miners all said they were going home and to leave Pyle alone. Bray had then called them soft and said he was going to pull out a rail from the fence and fell Pyle with it. The witnesses stated that Bray had been carrying nothing at that time. Later that evening Bray was seen with a parcel. One of the witnesses, George Race, stated that Bray had come home that evening with silver in his pocket saying that he 'had put a blackleg through'. Bray also had a parcel containing two shirts and he mentioned something about a jacket. He told Race to put the shirts in water. Race said he thought these had been stolen from Pyle and told Bray 'to bring nothing more'. Race then said he had later burned the shirts. Three days after this incident Race and Bray had argued, with Bray saying that Race had opened his mouth too much. And that he had better stay sober or he might find himself one night in the same situation as Pyle.

The defence asked why this information had not been forthcoming at the time of the murder. The witnesses all replied that Bray had threatened them with the same as had happened to Pyle if they said anything. The defence then asked if the information was now being given because of the £200 reward on offer. The witnesses denied that the reward had anything to do with them coming forward.

Bray denied the murder saying that the miners were committing perjury and that it was George Race who had threatened Pyle.

The jury believed the witnesses and Peter Bray was found guilty of murder. He was sent to meet his maker on 19 November 1883 by Justice Day. Bartholomew Binns carried out the hanging. Binns was sacked from his office of chief executioner within a year because there were so many complaints against him on his methods of execution. After his dismissal he was still employed to assist the appointed chief executioner.

Chapter 27

Attack at Spennymoor 1885

John Gould, a coke drawer, and his wife lived at Whitworth, Spennymoor. The couple had been together a number of years and seemed to have a happy relationship. In the same occupation as Gould and living nearby were William Wright and his wife. The two couples had a very close friendship but all that was to change on 24 February 1885.

A neighbour, Sarah Ellen Sammergill, was standing at her front door at about five thirty when she saw Wright enter Gould's house. About five minutes later Wright staggered into the street covered in blood. Gould came after him and it appeared to Sarah that the pair of them began wrestling for possession of an iron poker. Gould was trying to hit Wright in the face and Wright was trying to stop him. Sarah ran up the street shouting 'murder'. Wright staggered into a house in Craddock Street belonging to John Elliott. Elliott helped Wright to a chair and sent for the police. Gould came to the door and demanded that Elliott send Wright out so he could 'finish him'. Elliott refused saying he had known the man for nine years and that he was inoffensive. Gould replied that if Elliott knew what he knew he would throw Wright out of his house. The police then arrived and arrested Gould.

Dr R S Anderson had been called to attend to the injured man. There were two wounds to his head and Wright was complaining of severe pain in his abdomen. The doctor had him moved to his son's house in Viner Street where he administered a draught to ease the pain. When Dr Anderson saw his patient again the next day it was plain that he was much worse. The doctor told Wright there was nothing he could do for him and that he was dying. Wright then told the doctor that he wished to make a statement. Dr Anderson wrote the words as the dying man spoke them:

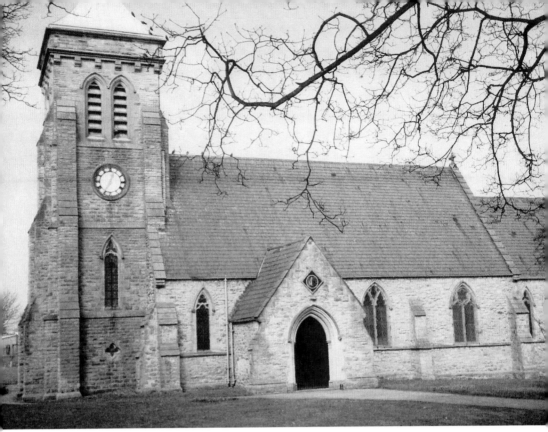

St Paul's Church in Spennymoor, 2003. The author

The individual wished to make his wife swear that I committed a rape upon her, which I can swear is not true. A week gone Saturday she said to my wife that she never knew a man but her own husband. I said that I had never interfered with her in any shape or form whatsoever. To get herself clear she said I had done so-and-so with her. Her husband never spoke to me about it and I never dreamt that he thought I would take advantage of her. He came on Sunday and was at our house again on Monday but never gave any hint. On Monday night when I went in I said to him 'the door's open, what's up' and he said 'you b...... I'll let you know what's up' then he brayed me with the poker. If God was to strike me down this minute I never interfered with her. I have no more to add.

An initial inquest was held at *The North Eastern* hotel in Spennymoor early in March. John Gould's niece, Elizabeth Gibbon, was called to give evidence. She stated that at Shildon flower show the previous year she had seen Mrs Gould in the company of Wright while her uncle was at work. Elizabeth did not mention it to anyone. On 14 February she had gone to the

Gould's house and said that when she opened the door Mrs Gould was lying on the mat in the kitchen with Wright kneeling on the floor about to kiss her. Elizabeth eventually told her uncle a few days before he attacked Wright.

The jury brought in a verdict of wilful murder and Gould was committed to trial at Durham Assizes.

Mr Milvain defended Gould and stated that the crime was not premeditated. His niece had told Gould on 23 February that his wife was being unfaithful. On the following night when Wright came to the house Gould assumed he was there to repeat the assault and, under extreme feelings of jealousy and provocation, he had attacked Wright. The jury found Gould guilty of manslaughter. The judge, in summing up, said that Gould had been ill-used by his wife and had taken the law into his own hands. He felt there was no doubt that he had meant to take Wright's life. A sentence of five years penal servitude was passed upon Gould.

This case is a prime example that a statement from one person alone, without further evidence, could sway the course of justice. It also shows that a hint of infidelity in a wife was not to be tolerated.

The North Eastern hotel in Spennymoor *where the initial inquest on John Gould was held.* The author

Chapter 28

Tragedy at Middlestone Moor
1902

Living at 25 Albion Street, Middlestone Moor was a miner, John Young, his wife Isabella, his stepdaughter Isabel Walton and her daughter, eleven months old Esther Jane Walton. Isabel had been living with her mother and stepfather since being separated from her husband, Samuel, in August. On 4 September the couple were legally separated on a magistrates order and Walton was instructed to pay 10s (50p) a week for the maintenance of his wife and child.

About noon on 11 September John Young was leaving his house to go into Spennymoor when he saw Walton walking across the field. Young assumed that Walton was coming to pay the first installment of the maintenance due. As the two were not on speaking terms, Young left the house before Walton reached the door. The tragic events that followed were related at the ensuing inquest held at the *Binchester Hotel* in the presence of Mr Proud, Coroner.

Dr R Anderson from Spennymoor had been passing through Middlestone Moor about one o'clock on 11 September. His carriage was stopped and he was told someone had been shot. On arriving at Albion Street there was a scene of utter carnage. The sight of two dead bodies greeted him. One was John Young's wife, Isabella, who had been shot through the eye; the other was their baby granddaughter, Esther, who had been shot in the head. Isabel Walton had been badly injured by a close range gunshot wound to the head and Samuel Walton had tried to cut his own throat. In Walton's pockets were about forty rounds of ammunition and his marriage certificate. On the back of the certificate he had written 'Mother gets all, signed Samuel Walton.' The doctor had Isabel taken to Auckland Hospital and after bandaging his wound had Samuel removed to Durham Hospital.

The County Hospital, Durham, opened in 1883. Author's collection

A neighbour had seen Isabel Walton talking to her husband just after noon on that terrible day. She held out her hand to him, probably for her money, the neighbour then heard Walton shout that 'he would swing for them'. At that there was a loud bang and a flash of light. More shots followed and Isabel had staggered to the doorway of the neighbour and said 'my mother is dead, my baby is dead and I am dying.'

A friend of Walton's, Arthur Crow, who resided with his father at the *Excelsior Hotel*, had let him stay at the hotel for a few days. Crow said that Walton had been very restless and upset. On 10 September Walton had told Crow that he was going to kill his family and then leave the country. His friend had told him not to be so foolish but did not really believe Walton's threat was serious.

Another witness said that a man fitting Walton's description had gone to a pawnshop in Tudhoe Grange and purchased a bulldog revolver and a box of fifty cartridges for 10s 6d. (53p)

The same evening Walton was in the *Mason's Arms* when he pulled out a revolver and said 'Tomorrow I've to pay my first 10s and I am likely to pay it with this'.

The jury did not even retire but immediately brought in a verdict of guilty. Walton was committed for trial to the Durham Assizes before Justice Channel. Between the two trials Isabel Walton also died from her wounds.

Walton's defence entered a plea for mercy on the grounds that Walton was upset at the breakup of his marriage and did not mean to kill anyone but himself. For an instant his personality had changed and he had become a lunatic. The prosecution stated that he had gone to a pawnshop and bought the gun and ammunition, had told his friend that he was going to kill his family, therefore, it was premeditated murder. The plea for mercy was ignored and he was again found guilty and sentenced to death. It was reported that when he was sentenced, he smiled.

Samuel Walton, thirty-one years of age, was hung for the triple murder on 16 December 1902. His executioners were William and John Billington.

The funerals of Esther and her grandmother were held together at Binchester Church on 13 September and Isabel Walton's funeral took place a few days later.

Chapter 29

By His Father's Hand
1903

Ernest Johnson was twenty-three and an idle, good for nothing. The family, consisting of the parents, seven children and a lodger, lived in a small house at 1 Suddick Street, Sunderland. Ernest's brother, John, was fifteen and earned 5s (25p) a week as a driver at the collieries. His wage and a little rent from the lodger was the only money coming in to support the family. Their forty-four year old father, Alfred, had worked as a shipwright but was unemployed and looking for work.

Things came to a head one Tuesday. Late in the afternoon Alfred spoke to Ernest about looking for work but Ernest lifted a chair and threatened to hit his father with it. Alfred left the house and later that evening came home drunk. Ernest was lying on the couch and his father started on him again about not looking for work. They began bickering and suddenly, in front of the family and the lodger, Alfred lunged at Ernest with an open pocketknife. The knife stuck into the left side of Ernest's head. John pushed his father aside and pulled the knife from his brother's head. Alfred then calmly walked out of the house. He went straight to PC Henderson, who was on duty on the Green at Southwick, and told him what he had done. Henderson went to the house and when he saw Ernest's condition, took Alfred into custody. On being charged with wounding his son Alfred said, 'It's all right. I hope the b...... dies. I did it and left the knife sticking in his head'.

Ernest was taken to Monkwearmouth Hospital where he died the following day. The charge against Alfred was now murder.

More than two years previously Ernest had been a private in the Northumberland Fusiliers. He had been imprisoned for twelve months and dismissed from the regiment for striking an officer. He had not worked since then and would tell his father that he would have to keep him. Ernest had also been in front of

Sedgefield Church in the eighteenth century. Author's collection

the borough bench fourteen times for different offences. In 1902 he had been convicted of larceny.

At the trial the family testified that Ernest had once attacked his father with a poker and would continually provoke him. They had an uncle who was in Morpeth Asylum because of insanity due to alcohol. Two cousins, also insane, were in Sedgefield Asylum. Justice Grantham asked John Johnson if Ernest was insane. John replied that his brother was 'queer' and that was why he would not work.

The jury found Alfred Johnson guilty of the murder of his son but with a strong recommendation for mercy. Justice Grantham pronounced the sentence of death. The Home Secretary heeded the plea for mercy and the sentence was commuted to life imprisonment.

Chapter 30

The Stonemason's Workshop 1904

Robert John Allen was a good-looking man who looked younger than his twenty years. He was the son of the gatekeeper of Durham prison and worked as an apprentice for Councilor Charles Lowes, a stonemason, at his Gilesgate workshop. Lowes was known for his violent temper towards his employees.

Allen was in bother for not putting in his full day's work one Saturday. The following day, Sunday, 9 July, his employer was determined for his apprentice to make up the lost time. After some dispute they reached an agreement whereby Allen would work an extra hour. When the normal workday had finished Lowes dismissed all the other apprentices except Allen, who stayed to make up his time. Allen was working in the stone yard for a time where a servant girl saw him. He then went to the upper story of the workshop where the office was situated.

Later that evening Lowes was found lying with his head over a tub. At least three blows with something heavy had been inflicted to his head, fracturing his skull and killing him. There were evident signs of a struggle, including a pile of marble slabs that had been overturned and broken.

The police went to Allen's house but he had taken the train to Sunderland. He returned at midnight the following Saturday and was promptly arrested. When questioned, Allen at first said that when he had left the workshop, there was a strange man there seeking work. When the police searched Allen's house they found his clothes, which were heavily bloodstained.

Allen eventually admitted to killing Lowes but said he was provoked as Lowes had struck him on more than one occasion. About eighteen months previously, Allen had gone to a solicitor with a view to charging Lowes with assault. Lowes had apologised so the charges had been dropped. Allen said that on the evening Lowes died he had tried to strike Allen with an iron bar. Allen had made a promise to himself that the next time Lowes laid his hands on him he would thrash him. He had taken the iron bar from Lowes and struck him with it. Allen could not remember how often he had struck Lowes and did not realise he had hit him hard enough to kill him. When Allen realised Lowes was dead, he panicked and ran out the back way. Going home first and changing his clothes he had then taken the train to Sunderland. William George Wright had worked at the stonemason's yard until his retirement three years before. He stated that Allen was telling the truth about Lowes and his violent temper. Wright had seen Lowes kick and hit Allen on numerous occasions.

The prosecution pointed out that there were no bruises on Allen and that Lowes had been hit more than once. Two more blows had been struck with extreme violence, probably after the man was already dead. Also Allen had run away, lied to the police and had not seemed repentant.

At the Durham Assizes before Justice Grantham the jury spent a long time trying to reach an agreement. They eventually returned a verdict of manslaughter. Justice Grantham stated that he felt the jury had taken a very compassionate view of the case. He thought that this was the most brutal murder he had ever heard of. Allen was then sentence to penal servitude for twenty years.

Chapter 31

A Burglary at the Co-op
1907

It was thought that a thief had targeted the Co-operative Store at Windy Nook on more than one occasion. It was suspected that meat that had been in the store when it closed in the evening was gone the following morning. A trap was set by sawdust being sprinkled on the floor of the butcher's department last thing at night. The following morning footprints were found leading across the sawdust, which confirmed the society committee's suspicions a thief had been targeting the store at nights. The committee decided to employ a few men to keep watch for two or three nights to try and catch the culprit. There was already talk that the thief was John William Noble, a blacksmith of the area. On the night of 31 October 1907, four men, George Ather, Christopher Carr, John Joseph Cowell and John Patterson were hired for the watch. Ather was positioned at one side of the office and the other three in the mincing room. Mr Sutton, manager of the butchering department, went through the usual form and locked the door of the store from the outside at about nine forty-five.

About one o'clock on the morning of 1 November the watchers saw the lamp of the policeman as he walked his beat, trying the door to make sure it was secure as he passed. At four o'clock the watchers saw another lamp outside. There was no sound of footsteps, but the door of the store was opened from the outside. Ather heard the key being removed from the outside lock and he could see the dim shape of a man as he entered. The man then locked the door from the inside, and with a lantern in one hand and what looked like a stick under his arm, made his way to the slaughterhouse. The shadowy figure then returned to the front of the store. Carr and Patterson came out from the mincing room with Cowell behind them. Carr and Patterson rushed at the man and got hold of him by the left side and Ather took hold of his right wrist. Cowell went to the door to turn on the light but could not get it to come on. A violent struggle took place in virtual darkness. The intruder was a large and powerful man and was obviously intent on not being overpowered. Carr let go his hold to pick up a butcher's steel from the counter. With this he hit the man twice on the back of the head. Cowell was coming back from the door when he suddenly shouted out 'He's got a revolver'. As Cowell shouted his warning, the man fired the weapon, the bullet hitting Patterson just above his left eye. The injured man fell to the floor just as the weapon was fired a second time, this time the bullet hitting Carr, wounding him quite seriously. Ather and Cowell were left struggling with a desperate and armed man in the dark. Common sense prevailed and the three men headed for the door, Ather grabbing a hammer as he left. Cowell went for the police while Ather and Carr held the door to try and keep the intruder in the store. Two men that were passing heard the commotion and one went to fetch Mrs Ather. As she was coming round the corner she heard someone try to break a window. She alerted her husband who ran to the window. A man was easing himself out of the broken window. Ather hit him twice with the hammer, once on the leg and once on the body but the man ran off and was soon out of sight. Patterson died within the hour.

When the police arrived they found a false beard, a cap and a stick. They believed the stick had been used to sabotage the lights. The three survivors, although the store had been dark, felt sure that the intruder was, as they suspected, John Noble. On a search being made of Noble's house new blankets, sheets and rolls of material were found in two sets of drawers. Under the bed were tins of mustard, boot polish and tablets of soap. Some of the goods were marked Co-operative Wholesale Society. There was also a set of keys for the store. Noble was arrested for the crimes and sentenced to death for wilful murder by Justice Channell. At first there was anger and contempt for the murderer but after the sentencing the feelings changed to sympathy for Noble's wife and family. There was speculation as to why the police had not been called in by the management committee of the store to handle the situation when theft was suspected. Also why did the men not alert the local policeman when he tried the door to make sure it was secure? If this had been done Noble would probably only have been charged with shop breaking and the shooting would never have taken place.

A petition was sent to the Home Secretary with a plea to reprieve the condemned man but it was denied. The brothers Henry and Thomas Pierrepoint carried out the execution on 24 March 1908. Robert Lawman was also executed for murder on the same day. It was the first execution at Durham for four years and the first double execution for six years.

Chapter 32

A Double Murder at Darlington 1907

lbert Hill in Darlington was once notorious for brawls and domestic violence. Steel forges and engineering works merged in with small houses built for the working classes. Life was hard for many families and over indulgence in drink was common. Depression, although largely unrecognised as such, would have been an illness that many would have suffered. John Hanlon was twenty-six years old and well known for his skills at football. He worked as a striker at Gummerson's Engineering Works in Darlington. In modern times Hanlon would probably have been diagnosed a depressive.

One Sunday in November 1907, Hanlon calmly locked the door of his house at 43 Grey Street, Albert Hill and made his way to a house in Vulcan Street. Handing his door key to the occupier of the house, Miss Morrow, he said to her 'he had done it'. The startled girl asked Hanlon what it was he had done and he told her he had killed his sister and the mother of his two

Tubwell Row, Darlington in 1905. Author's collection

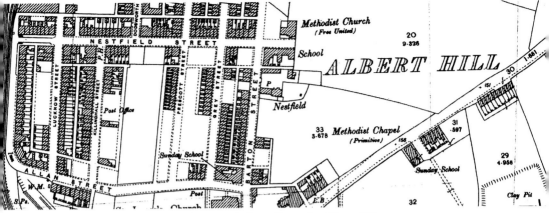

A map showing Vulcan Street and Grey Street in Albert Hill. Ordnance Survey, Darlington 1898.

children. Hanlon then started describing a double murder in graphic detail. In utter disbelief Miss Morrow rushed to Hanlon's house, unlocked the door and looked in. The scene of carnage that she saw sent her screaming into the street.

The police quickly made their way to the house. In the front parlour they found the bodies of two young women. One was seventeen year-old Catherine Hanlon usually known as Kate; the other was twenty-two year old Margaret Dickenson. The trail of blood gave witness to the fact that Kate had been brutally murdered while she was in the pantry. Her throat had been cut and with her head almost severed from her body, she had been dragged through the house and into the parlour. Margaret had been strangled and the two young women's bodies had been left to lie beside each other.

At the same time the police were at the scene of the crime, Hanlon was walking near some forge works when he met a young lady he was acquainted with. He said to her 'goodbye Florrie, I've done it'. He then walked into the crowd that gathered outside the house in Grey Street and asked what had happened.

Hanlon was formally charged with causing the deaths of the two women and was initially brought up before the magistrates at Darlington. He seemed ill and confused and did not seem to remember what he had done. No one who knew Hanlon, his sister and Margaret could shed light on why he had carried out the murders. There was no bad feeling between them that was known of and it was generally thought that Hanlon had acted on some sort of mad impulse.

The case continued on into 1908 and eventually it was ordered that Hanlon be medically examined so as to determine

High Row, Darlington in the early twentieth century. Author's collection

his sanity. He was declared insane and he was locked up where he could hurt no one else.

Margaret was buried at the west cemetery and Kate at the north. Sixty women carrying white chrysanthemums preceded the hearse carrying Kate's body. They were members of the St William's branch of the Children of Mary of which Kate had been a member.

St William's Church, Darlington. The author

Chapter 33

A Shooting at Chopwell
1909

Abel Atherton was a thirty-year old miner. He had been lodging for some time with the Patrick family. Mrs Elizabeth Ann Patrick was thirty-three and married to a miner. They had a daughter, Frances Mary, who was fifteen. Atherton, for some time, had been making improper suggestions to Frances and she threatened to complain to her parents if he did not stop. Eventually, he had tried to kiss her and Frances told her parents about his attentions saying that if Atherton did not leave the house she would. Mr Patrick spoke to the lodger and told him to leave. Atherton moved near by into Mrs Isabella Forster's house but he frequently visited the Patrick's house and began making allegations that it was Frances who had led him on and that they had been intimate at her request. On 11 August Atherton called at the house and again made charges of misconduct against Francis. Mrs Patrick ordered him from the house telling him not to return.

That evening Atherton returned to the Patrick's house a little worse for drink and carrying a gun in his arms with the muzzle pointing to the ground. Mrs Patrick, Frances and a neighbour, Mrs Marley, were present when he arrived at the back door. Mrs

Chopwell Colliery. Durham Mining Museum

Chopwell. Author's collection

Patrick told him to put the gun down as she felt he was holding it in a threatening manner. After that there was confusion. Mrs Patrick seized the gun by the barrel and she ended up outside with Atherton. Frances tried to follow them out but was held back by Mrs Marley. As Mrs Patrick tried to pull the gun from Atherton a shot was heard and then a few seconds later the gun fired again. When Frances and Mrs Marley went outside Mrs Patrick was lying on the footpath where she died within minutes. Atherton took a knife from his pocket and tried to cut his throat but merely managed to inflict a scratch.

Atherton was arrested and stood trial at Durham Assizes before Judge Walton. Thirty-eight pellets were extracted from

Mrs Patrick's body during the post-mortem. The accused man stated that the whole thing was an accident. Mrs Patrick had taken the gun and fired one shot into the air and then shot herself. He also said that he had tried to stop her but that Frances and Mrs Marley had held him back. When asked why he had the gun in the first place, Atherton said he had been going to sell it and had only stopped at the Patrick's house to frighten them with it. He kept insisting that Frances had led him on. Mrs Forster, with whom Atherton had lodged after leaving the Patrick's house, told the court that on 24 July Atherton had shown her three cartridges saying one was for Mr Patrick, one for Frances and one for himself. On the day of the shooting Atherton had taken his gun and told Mrs Forster he was going to have a bit of sport. Before leaving the house he had shaken both her and her daughter's hand and began to cry. Mrs Forster had asked what was the matter but Atherton did not reply. Medical evidence was brought in to show that Atherton's allegations against Frances saying that they had been intimate were untrue. Abel Atherton was sentenced to death for the wilful murder of Elizabeth Ann Patrick and was hanged by Henry Pierrepoint on 8 December 1908.

Chronology

Durham has had a long and, sometimes violent and bloody history. Some of these events are recorded in full and give a very factual record. Others have not been written in their entirety and the full chain of events is now lost in the mists of time. Religion and superstition played their parts in unnecessary deaths. This is a short chronology of some of the foul deeds that have taken place over the centuries.

c1070: William I, in the harrying of the North

> *wasted all the faire countrie betwixt Yorke and Durham, leaving all desolate for three score miles space, which nine years after laid untilled with scarcely any inhabitants, when grew so great a famine these northerns were forced to eat the flesh of men.*

1511, 24 March: John Bulman of Blakwell begged sanctuary at Durham Cathedral for having, thirteen years before, in the house of William Bulman, feloniously struck one N Walley with a dagger in the breast, of which wound he died two days later.

Durham Cathedral. Author's collection

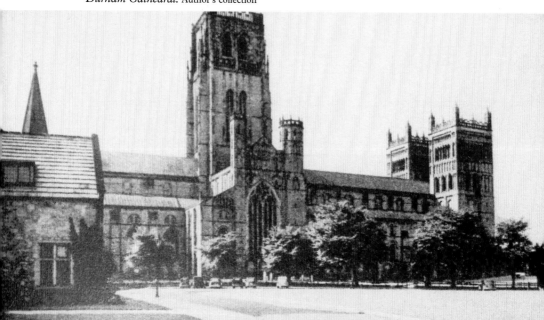

1590, 27 May: Four priests were hanged and quartered at Durham 'for their horryble offence'. Their names were Hill, Hogge, Holiday and Duke. Legend has it that a stream near to the gallows dried up at the time of their execution and never flowed again, hence the name Dryburn.

1592, 8 August: In the parish register of St Nicholas are written the names of five men. Simson, Arrington, Fetherstone, Fenwicke and Lanckaster. These men were hanged because it was 'thought' they were Egyptians. (Gypsies)

1594, 4 February: John Speed, a layman, was executed at Durham for aiding Roman Catholic priests.

1594, 24 July: John Boast, a Roman Catholic priest, was executed at Durham for practising his religion. Two other priests were condemned at the same time. John Ingram was hanged at Gateshead. George Swallowell was hung, drawn and quartered at Darlington.

The River Skerne, Darlington. The author

1597, 26 August: Anthony Arrowsmith, arraigned of murder at Durham, stood mute upon his trial and was pressed to death in Durham market place.

1652, January: Two men, Adamson and Powle, were executed at Durham for practicing witchcraft.

1668, July: At Durham Assizes, Alice Armstrong, wife of Christopher, a labourer of Shotton, was tried for bewitching to death an ox belonging to Barbara Thompson. The sentence was not recorded.

Seaton Carew in 1853, photo taken by James Backhouse. Pattison's Pictures, Bowes Museum

1673, 5 October: At Seaton Carew John Harrison, a cripple, murdered Thomas Smailes, a glazier, with his crutch. Harrison was executed at Durham for his crime.

1711, 13 August: Thomas Wilson, John Brady, Andrew Miller, Andrew Langland and Robert Evans were executed at Durham for breaking into the house of William Storey, a miller, and stealing 10 guineas in gold and £59.5s in money. (£69.75p)

1725, August: An attempt was made to poison William Coatsworth of Park House, Gateshead, by putting arsenic in his chocolate. His butler and gardener, John Brown and Christopher Richardson were found guilty at Durham. One was sentenced to five and one to three years. On 10 June, which was the day the crime was committed, during every year of their confinement they were to be whipped ten times around the market place. In addition, on the Saturday following the quarter sessions for the peace they were to stand in the pillory.

Gateshead in the nineteenth century. Author's collection

1726, 3 August: Stephen Browne, Arthur Hewetson, David Steel, Ann Bone and Jane Brown were executed at Durham for stealing 32 guineas (£33.60p) from John Marshall on the King's highway.

1727, July: William Stephenson, a grocer of Northallerton, was hanged at Durham for the murder of Mary Farding, who was pregnant by him. She was thrown into the sea at Hartlepool near the rock formation known as the Maiden's Bower. In the churchwarden's accounts dated June 7, 1727 a charge of 1s 10d (11p) was written in as unpaid 'for making Mary Farthing's grave'.

Maiden's Bower, rock formation at Hartlepool. Author's collection

1732, 18 May: John Graham and James Graham, two notorious offenders, were executed at Durham for horse stealing. James Graham was baptised on the morning of his execution, at the church of St Mary-le-Bow, a part of the old gaol being within that parish.

1735, October: A child of James and Elizabeth Leesh, of Chester-le-Street, was played for at cards, at the sign of the *Salmon*. One game, four shillings (20p) against the child, by Henry and John Trotter, Robert Thomson and Thomas Ellison, which was won by the latter, and the child was delivered to him accordingly.

1739, 25 April: Thomas Galilee was executed at Durham for horse stealing. He confessed to having committed the same crime on many previous occasions.

1741, 17 April: At Fishburn near Sedgefield, a woman named Charlton used a meat cleaver to kill her fourteen-year old son and two younger children. She then stabbed herself behind the ear and died instantly. The slaughter took place while her husband was occupied with trying to get a cow out of a ditch. The verdict was lunacy.

1748, 15 August: Paul Coleman, a desperate fellow upwards of six feet high, was executed at Durham on this date for a robbery on Elvet Moor. His victim was Mr Hutchinson, an attorney of Durham. He had taken Mr Hutchinson's watch and other possessions including his horse. The horse was found near Plawsworth. On searching Coleman's lodgings, pistols, slugs, flints and powder were found. It was believed he had come north from London with the express purpose of housebreaking and highway robbery.

1753, 24 January: A wealthy merchant of Sunderland, Mr William Maud, did not return home after carrying out some business in South Shields. His horse was found near to where he was last seen. Maud's body was found on 22 March in a runner of water near Boldon. His widow, two of his associates and His Majesty, George II, all offered 50 guineas (£52.50) reward for the apprehension of the murderers but to no avail.

1753, 30 September: Two young men knocked on a door in Darlington. It was the house of a dyer, Mr Moncaster. They asked if they could speak to his daughter. On being refused permission, the men forced the door open and beat Mr Moncaster so severely with their whips that he died.

1763, Monday 1 August: Margaret Middleton, alias Coulson, was executed at Durham for the murder of a bastard child, Lucy Elliott, alias Curry. Margaret had been paid a considerable amount of money by a township of Durham to take the child to Northallerton and to bring her up. Margaret took the child only as far as the River Browney, about two miles from Durham, and drowned her there on 24 June.

1766, 14 September: A person named Christopher Hull, two shoemakers, named Rippon, and a weaver, in company together at a public house, at Wolviston, near Stockton, Durham, having quarrelled, went out to the fields to fight. Hull received a stab in the heart with a knife, which killed him on the spot. At the Assizes held at Durham in August 1767, James and John Rippon were tried for the murder of Hull, found guilty and burnt in the hand.

1783, 18 August: Robert Storey was executed at Durham for the murder of Thomas Idle. He had waylaid him for the purpose of robbery and murder. Thomas was known as 'Cockle Geordy' because he was a cockle seller.

1785, 25 July: John Winship, a farmer from Monkwearmouth, was executed at Durham. He had poisoned his maidservant by giving her drugs to procure an abortion. His body was given to a surgeon at Sunderland, Mr Wilkinson, for dissection.

1789, June: Buried in the mud in a burn near Ebchester the body of a child was found by some boys who were fishing. A stake had been driven through the body into the earth. This was the third child to be found dead within a few months in that neighbourhood. As there were no commissioners of the peace in the area investigations were never carried out as to whom the perpetrators were.

1789, November: Jane Ramshaw was decoyed at night from her house in the City of Durham and horribly murdered. No one was apprehended for the crime but there was a rumour that a soldier, when on his deathbed on the continent, confessed to the crime.

1790, 18 August: John Brown for housebreaking, James Greenwood for shop breaking and George Bolton for horse stealing were executed at Morpeth. Brown was from Winlaton and had a wife and six children. Greenwood had a wife and three children and Bolton was a servant from Usworth. The triple execution brought a huge crowd of spectators.

1816, 17 August: John Grieg was the first to be hanged on the drop before the new courthouse. He had murdered Elizabeth Stonehouse. Prior to this executions took place at Dryburn near Framwellgate Moor.

1836, 20 February: Richard Taylor a seventy-six year old shoemaker was brutally murdered in Lumley. Two boys found his body. Taylor's head had been beaten until almost flat and his brains were scattered about the ground. He had been robbed of between ten and twenty shillings. (50p-£1) The perpetrators were never apprehended.

An old sketch of Monkwearmouth. Author's collection

1840, 29 June: Robert Taylor, alias Lord Kennedy, was tried and convicted on a charge of bigamy. Six marriages had come to the knowledge of the police but it was thought the number was greater. He received two and a half years imprisonment. Amazingly, his age was only nineteen!

1842, 22 February: James Liddle was a foreman at Edward Lumsdon and Son, Strand Street, Monkwearmouth. When Liddle remonstrated with a workman, James Robertson, for neglecting his work, the consequences were dire. Robertson lifted a sledgehammer and struck Liddle a tremendous blow on the head. Liddle died the next morning from a severely fractured skull. Robertson was tried at the Durham Summer Assizes before Lord Denham, found guilty and sentenced to transportation for life.

1842, 26 July: The body of a brutally murdered young woman was found on the seashore near Hardwicke. She was eventually identified as Jane Jackson, daughter of a respectable man from Easington.

1844, 11 November: Matthew and James Watson, Henry Russell and D Buglass were committed to Durham gaol to take their trial for forgery and issuing forged notes of the Stockton and Durham Bank. The trial took place on 19 December and they were found guilty. Buglass was sentenced to fifteen years transportation, Russell and Matthew Watson to twenty. James Watson's sentence was remitted as he came forward as a witness.

1845, 10 June: Mr Louis Henry Goule, a superintendent of rural police, saw his wife in the company of a gentleman in Church Street in Durham. Goule fired two pistols at his wife breaking her arm in two places. He then attacked her escort, Mr Walter Scruton, deputy clerk of the peace. With the butt end of his pistol Goule inflicted considerable injuries to Scruton's head. Goule was arrested and while in custody tried unsuccessfully to cut his throat with a penknife. Mrs Goule died of her injuries and her husband was tried before Baron Rolfe for murder. Goule was acquitted on the grounds of insanity.

Durham Castle in 2003. The author

Sources

1. Robert Surtees, *The History and Antiquities of the County Palatine of Durham*, Volume II, 1820.

2. John Sykes, *Local Records of Remarkable Events which have occurred in Northumberland and Durham, Newcastle Upon Tyne and Berwick Upon Tweed*, Volumes I-III, 1833.

3. T Fordyce, *Local Records of Remarkable Events which occurred in Northumberland and Durham, Newcastle Upon Tyne and Berwick Upon Tweed*, Volumes III-IV, 1876. A continuation of the work published by John Sykes.

4. Longstaffe, *The History and Antiquities of Darlington*, 1854.

5. M A Richardson, *The Borderer's Table Book on Gatherings of the Local History and Romance of the English and Scottish Border*, Volumes I-VIII, 1846.

6. Reid's *Handbook to Newcastle*, 1863.

7. William Brockie, *Legends and Superstitions of the County of Durham*, Sunderland 1866.

8. T Richmond, *Local History of Stockton and Neighbourhood*, 1868.

9. *Haydn's Dictionary of Dates*, London, 1895.

10. *Hartlepool Free Press.*

11. *The Sunderland News and North of England Advertiser.*

12. *Stockton and Hartlepool Mercury and Middlesbrough News.*

13. *Stockton and Cleveland Mercury.*

14. *South Durham Herald.*

15. *South Durham Herald and Stockton Journal.*

16. *Northern Daily Mail.*

17. *Durham Advertiser.*

Index